SO-AET-886

the
CONVERSION
OF
ST. PAUL

HERALD SCRIPTURAL LIBRARY
Robert J. Karris O.F.M., General Editor

the CONVERSION OF ST. PAUL:

Narrative and History in Acts

by

Gerhard Lohfink

●

translated and edited

by Bruce J. Malina

FRANCISCAN HERALD PRESS
1434 WEST 51st STREET ● CHICAGO. 60609

The Conversion of St. Paul by Gerhard Lohfink, translated from the German of Paulus vor Damaskus, 3d. ed. 1967, Verlag Katholisches Bibelwerk GmbH., Silberburgstrasse 121a, D-7 Stuttgart 1, West German Republic. © Copyright 1976 by Franciscan Herald Press, 1434 West 51st Street, Chicago, Illinois 60609. All Rights reserved. Made in the United States of America.

Library of Congress Cataloging in Publication Data:

Lohfink, Gerhard, 1934-
    The conversion of St. Paul.

    (Herald scriptural library)
    Translation of Paulus vor Damaskus, 3d. ed. (1967)
    Bibliography: p.
    1. Paul, Saint, apostle. 2. Bible. N.T. Acts—
Criticism, interpretation, etc. I. Title.
BS2506.L5713   225.9'24 [B]   75-12796
ISBN 0-8199-0572-0

NIHIL OBSTAT:
Mark Hegener O.F.M.
    Censor

IMPRIMATUR:
    Msgr. Richard A. Rosemeyer, J.D.
Vicar General, Archdiocese of Chicago

January 15, 1976

Contents

Preface

This book is based upon a series of lectures which I gave at the beginning of the year to religious educators in Frankfurt. I expanded these lectures for publication, mainly by adding more examples and illustrations. The chapter on "The Apparition Dialogue" (III, 2) includes material subsequently published in the *Biblische Zeitschrift* (1965), and I believe it contains something new in the world of biblical scholarship. Otherwise, I feel obligated to confess my gratitude to the many contributors to research on Acts, and especially on the Lukan Damascus story. From the vast amount of material in this area, I would like to single out one work for special mention, namely, the commentary on the Acts of the Apostles by Ernst Haenchen. This work has opened up a new field of investigation into Acts. And without this far-reaching and stimulating commentary, the following work would not have been possible.

Würzburg, June 30, 1965

Gerhard Lohfink

Translator's Note

This translation has been made from the third edition of Lohfink's *Paulus vor Damaskus.* The translation of Acts 9:1-19; 22:3-21; 26:9-19 has been made from the original Greek, and the idea of putting these texts in columns for comparison of content is the translator's. All other biblical texts are taken from the RSV, except where the Septuagint translation is called for.

Editing consisted mostly in adding appropriate texts and notes from Vatican II and references to the American situation in Catholic biblical scholarship.

Bruce J. Malina

Introduction

For a decade or so before the Second Vatican Council, the biblical movement in the Catholic Church evidenced a perceptible ground swell. Interest in the Bible and publications dealing with the Bible grew apace. And at the Second Vatican Council itself, new biblical perspectives received clear emphasis in at least two documents: the dogmatic constitution on divine revelation *(Dei Verbum)*[1] and the constitution on the sacred liturgy *(Sacrosanctum Concilium).*[2] Further, the reading and study of the Bible receive annual endorsement by the Catholic bishops of the United States during the presidentially proclaimed National Bible Week.

Although it cannot be said that the renewed emphasis on and publicity about the Bible has triggered enthusiasm in wide circles of Catholics, yet interest in the Bible has grown. One might even safely predict that in the near future, more Catholics than ever before will be reading the Bible. And even those who might not actually pick up a Bible in the future will soon become acquainted with a considerable number of biblical texts about which they were previously ignorant due to the wide selection of texts in the new lectionary used at Mass.

However, such broadened exposure to the Bible does entail a problem. The Catholic of the '70's perceives what he reads in the Bible with an entirely different set of persuppositions than did his forebearers in the 19th century. His general educational level is higher and broader, his historical scepticism greater. He has greater possibilities for comparing ideas and for gaining critical distance. Thus by and large the Bible fills the general reader with misgivings and apprehensions, even if he cannot exactly express his difficulties. [3]

It would· therefore be rather shortsighted to recommend the reading of the Bible to Catholics today without at the same time familiarizing them with the current methods and achievements of modern biblical scholarship. [4] For biblical scholars have for a long time critically investigated those aspects of the Bible which are apt to cause problems for the general Bible reader.

For example, take the commonly raised objection: "Did it really happen just as the Bible says? How could the biblical author have possibly known that?" Biblical scholars have considered and reflected upon such questions for many years now, though perhaps in terms of their own jargon. One result of this scholarly reflection which has generally prevailed in contemporary biblical study is insight concerning the nature of the *literary forms of expression* and *styles of literary composition* found in the Bible. The general Bible reader's habit of posing questions in *either-or* terms ("either it happened or it didn't happen") simply closes off access to most of the narrative texts of Sacred Scripture. For there are many varieties of historical truth falling between the extremes of *"either historical or not historical,"* and it is with these varieties that the general reader must become fully acquainted. Otherwise, reading the Bible will prove to be a source of continual difficulty and disillusionment.

To put it another way, I believe that *form-critical thinking* [5] ought not be reserved for professional biblical scholars but should become the common knowledge of every Bible reader.

Impossible? I would say that it is possible to the same extent that it was possible for the ordinary Christian to realize that the "Christian" heaven, viewed theologically, is not to be though of in a crass spatial sense, i.e., as located above the stars or beyond the Milky Way.

The foregoing discussion basically sketches out the theme of this volume. It deals with the literary forms used in the composition of biblical texts and with the historical truth of the Bible. But the theme is not going to be discussed abstractly, in outer space so to say; rather it will be considered in terms of some concrete texts of the Bible. To this end, I have chosen the story of the call and conversion of Paul, so amply told for us by the author of the Acts of the Apostles (henceforth simply, Acts).

Now I think it appropriate to offer a brief legitimation for my selection of these particular texts. Really, any text of the Bible could be used to demonstrate the form-critical method of contemporary exegesis—a psalm, a prophetic oracle, a Paul-line letter, etc. But for a presentation such as I envision, a narrative text is most appropriate since one will see the method at work in a most graphic way.[6] And to choose from among the various New Testament narrative texts means to pick a text from Acts or the four Gospels. In the past several years, Catholic biblical scholars have produced a series of good contributions to gospel research which demonstrate and discuss the form-critical method as applied to the gospel documents.[7] But as far as I can tell, such contributions are notably lacking in the area of Acts, although in fact "research into Acts in recent years has made rapid progress."[8] Furthermore, form-criticism applies differently to Acts than it does to the gospels, and the results the method yields in Acts research likewise differ from those in gospel research. For these reasons, I find it more challenging to delve into Acts.

Among the narratives of Acts, the call of Paul forms a

sort of high point, along with the Pentecost events and the Cornelius story. A cursory reading of the book points this up by the fact that this call is told not less than three times, specifically in chapters 9, 22 and 26. Because of this retelling by the author of Acts, we are afforded important opportunities for comparing seemingly similar texts. Besides, Paul himself writes about his call to be an apostle in several passages of his letters. Our comparison, therefore, can be extended to the Pauline letters as well.

Although we limit ourselves to a study of the call of Paul, and thus confine ourselves to well-defined and specific texts within the N.T., yet not even these texts can be treated exhaustively in this short work. In what follows, we shall not offer a line by line explanation of the texts in question, nor shall we deal with all of the problems of fact which the call of Paul entail. For example, we shall omit entirely the question of Paul's psychological readiness for his call, which formerly was much discussed. Rather our intention is to investigate the texts of Acts in specimen fashion, and this from the viewpoint of the *literary form of the presentation and historical truth.*

The outline of this work derives from the subject matter. First we shall present the texts themselves and focus upon the problems they pose (I). Then we shall describe the older interpretations of the Damascus story (II). Obviously this description cannot be complete here; we offer it rather to sketch out the background against which the methods of contemporary biblical interpretation operate and from which they stand out. Illustration of these last named features will then comprise the major part of this work (III).

I.

The Texts
and
The Problems They Pose

1. Acts 9:1-19; 22:3-21; 26:9-18.

The first time Paul is mentioned in Acts is at the story of Stephen's stoning. The witnesses to the incident lay down their garments at the feet of a young man named Saul (7:58b). Luke concludes his account of Stephen's martyrdom with the observation: "And Saul was consenting to his death" (8:1a). Right after this, Luke sets down a short summary dealing with the persecution which now broke out against the Church: "And on that day a great persecution arose against the church in Jerusalem; and they were all scattered throughout the region of Judea and Samaria, except the apostles." Saul plays the decisive role in this persecution: "But Saul laid waste the church, and entering house after house, he dragged off men and women and committed them to prison. Now those who were scattered went about preaching the word" (8:1b-4).

After this description of the new situation of persecution—the summary likewise marks the expansive movement of the Church beyond Jerusalem (cf. 1:8)—the activity of the deacon Philip is reported (8:5-13, 26-40). In the meantime the reader is left to linger under the impression made by 8:3; Paul continues his house to house search and the persecution rages on.[9] And it is precisely in this context that the author inserts the remark: "But Saul, *still* breathing threats and murder against the disciples of the Lord . . ." (9:1). Saul is now equipped with letters of authorization from Jewish officialdom and finds himself on the road to Damascus, intent upon seeking out Christians in that city as well.[10]

After a brief introduction (9:1,2), Luke reports the event proper. Near the city, a light from heaven suddenly flashes about the persecutor, and a voice addresses him: "Saul, Saul, why do you persecute me?" The way in which the name of the addressee is written here in Greek (Saoul) indicates that Hebrew is being spoken.[11] Luke in other places has "Saulos," or from 13:9 on, "Paulos."[12] The persecutor falls to the ground and is blinded by the brilliant light.[13] The one who addresses Saul in Hebrew from out of the brilliant light, is the exalted Lord. It is he who is persecuted when Saul persecutes the Christian community.

In the brief dialogue with Jesus, Saul utters but a single sentence: "Who are you, Lord?" (9:5). There is no opposition of any sort on Saul's part. With strong contrasting effect, Luke then describes how the one who so recently "breathed threats and murder" (9:1) must now be led by the hand by his travelling companions (9:8). Luke does not mention who these companions were. Perhaps he has a caravan in mind; Saul would have joined such a caravan for the trip to Damascus.

Be that as it may, Saul is led even deeper into the dark since Jesus left him in uncertainty as to further particulars: "Enter the city, and you will be told what you are to do" (9:6). Saul waits there three days, blind and fasting. Then the scene changes. We are told of a disciple named Ananias who apparently lives in Damascus with other Jewish Christians (cf. 9:19b). In a vision from Christ, this Ananias receives the task of seeking out Saul in a dwelling, the location of which is exactly described, and of laying his hands upon him. He is also told in this vision that Saul himself has seen him (Ananias) in a vision coming in and laying his hands upon him. Thus Luke presents us with a complicated and interwoven double vision.

In his answer to the Lord, Ananias is full of misgivings.

He had previously heard of Saul. With Ananias' hesitations, the reader is once more clearly apprised of how dangerous Saul had become for the Church, and what a colossal change was under way there outside Damascus.[14] Through Christ Ananias now learns what God intends with this change—and the reader too now learns it for the first time: Saul is destined to witness to the name of Christ among Gentiles and Jews. We are then told briefly how Ananias carries out Christ's command; he goes to Saul, heals, and baptizes him.

We now pass over the chapters of Acts which tell of how Paul, as "chosen instrument" (9:15), declares the word of God first to the Jews (9:20ff.; cf. 26:20), then to the Gentiles. Luke impressively describes how the gospel is carried to Asia Minor by Paul (chapters 13,14), and from there to Europe (chapters 16–18). Paul's last trip to Jerusalem marks a decisive turning point in his missionary activity (chapter 21). Diaspora Jews from Asia Minor cause a riot in the temple area in opposition to Paul; and he escapes with his life only by the quick intervention of Roman soldiers. In this situation, Paul makes a speech in his own defense before the Jews (22:1–21). What is striking about this speech is that Paul does not even go into the accusation of his profaning the temple; for it was this accusation that provided his opponents with the occasion to apprehend him (cf. 21:28, 29). Rather, by presenting his autobiography, Paul basically demonstrates that the mission to the Gentiles was willed by God himself. At this juncture, the Damascus story is told for the second time in Acts. But Paul cannot complete his speech because his mention of the Gentile mission sends his Jewish audience into a fit of rage. Luke describes the scene very vividly: they yell out, tear their garments and throw dust into the air (22:22,23).

In Acts 26 the Damascus story is told for the third

time. Once again the context is Paul making a speech of
self-defense, this time before the Roman procurator, Festus,
and the Jewish king, Agrippa, with his entourage. Paul
mentions his activity among Jews and Gentiles; and this
time, too, he is interrupted, and by Festus at that, who
cuts him off with the remark: "Paul, you are mad!"(26:24).

At this point, it would be useful to read the full texts
of the Damascus accounts. They are translated as literally
as possible so that the oft-noted Old Testament style of
Luke may be better apparent. And the texts are presented
here synoptically so that they may be compared for similarities and dissimilarities.[15]

Translated Texts
of the
Damascus Accounts

Notes   Acts 9:1-19

Acts 22:1-21

¹"Men, brothers and fathers,
listen to my defense now
before you."
² And when they heard that he
was talking to them in the
Hebrew language, they fell
all the more silent.
And he said:

³"I am a Jewish man, born
in Tarsus of Cilicia, but
brought up in this city at
the feet of Gamaliel, edu-
cated according to the
strictness of the law of
the Fathers, being a zealous
man for God, just like all
of you are today,

Acts 26:2-23

²"About all that I am accused
of by the Jews, O King Agrippa,
I consider myself fortunate in
making my defense before you
today, ³especially since you
are acquainted with all the
customs and controversies of
the Jews.
Therefore I pray to hear me out
patiently.
⁴All Jews know, then, my manner
of life from youth, spent from
the beginning with my nation
and at Jerusalem, ⁵fully aware
about me from the outset, if they
should like to attest to it, that
according to the strictest sect
of our religion, I lived as a
Pharisee. ⁶ And presently I stand
on trial concerning the hope of
the promise made by God to our
Fathers, ⁷in the fulfillment of
which our twelve tribes, worship-
ping sedulously night and day,
continue to hope. Concerning this
hope I am accused by the Jews,
O King. ⁸Why is it judged
incredible by any of you, whether
God raises the dead?

¹ And Saul, still breathing
threats and murder against
the disciples of the Lord,
went to the high priest and
² asked of him letters for
Damascus, to the synagogues,
so that if he should find
anyone being of the Way,
men as well as women, he
might lead them off bound
to Jerusalem.

³ And as he journeyed along,
it came to pass that he was
nearing Damascus when suddenly a light from heaven
flashed about him.

⁴ And when he fell to the
ground, he heard a voice
saying to him:

Saul, Saul, why do you persecute me?

⁵ And he said: Who are you,
Lord?

⁴who persecuted this Way to the death, binding and handing over into prison both men as well as women, ⁵ just as the high priest and the whole class of elders bear me witness. And when I received from them letters to the brothers, I was travelling to Damascus to lead back those being there bound to Jerusalem so that they might be punished.

⁶And it came to pass as I was travelling and drawing near to Damascus about noon that a great light from heaven suddenly flashed about me.

⁷And I fell all the way down and I heard a voice speaking to me:

Saul, Saul, why do you persecute me?

⁸And I answered: Who are you Lord?

⁹On this score I myself thought it was necessary to do many contrary things against the name of Jesus of Nazareth, ¹⁰and this I did in Jerusalem, and I locked up many of the saints in prisons, having received the authority from the high priests, and when it concerned their being put to death, I voted against them. ¹¹ And when I often sought their punishment throughout all synagogues, I used to force them to blaspheme, and raging furiously against them, I used to persecute them even into outlying cities. ¹²Under these conditions, when travelling to Damascus with the authority and commission of the high priests, ¹³in the middle of the day I saw, O King, along the road a light from heaven exceeding the brilliance of the sun shining about me and those travelling with me.

¹⁴And when we all fell down to the ground, I heard a voice saying to me in the Hebrew language:
Saul, Saul, why do you persecute me?
It is hard for you to kick against the goads.
¹⁵And I said: Who are you, Lord?

And he: I am Jesus whom you
are persecuting.

[6] But get up and go into the
city, and you will be told
what you must do.

[7] And the men traveling along
with him stood speechless,
hearing the voice, but seeing
no one.
[8] And Saul got up from the
ground. And having opened his
eyes, he saw nothing. And
leading him by the hand, they
brought him into Damascus.

And he said to me: I am
Jesus of Nazareth whom you
are persecuting.
⁹ And those who were with me
saw the light, but did not
hear the voice of the one
speaking to me.
¹⁰ And I said: What shall I do,
Lord? And the Lord said to me:
Get up and get going to Damascus, and there it shall be
told you about all that has
been determined for you to do.

And the Lord said: I am Jesus
whom you are persecuting.

¹⁶ But get up and stand on your
feet. For I have appeared to
you to appoint you as servant
and witness to the things in which
you saw me and to the things in
which I shall appear to you,
¹⁷ delivering you from the people
and from the Gentiles to whom I
am sending you, ¹⁸ to open their
eyes so that they may turn from
darkness to light and from the
authority of Satan to God, that
they may receive forgiveness of
sins and a share among those who
have been made holy, by faith in
me.

¹¹ And as I did not see due to
the brightness of that light,
being led by the hand by those
who were with me, I went into
Damascus.

⁹ And for three days he was
sightless, and he neither
ate nor drank.
¹⁰ And there was a certain disciple in Damascus by the name
of Ananias, and the Lord said
to him in a vision: Ananias!
And he said: Here I am, Lord.
¹¹ And the Lord to him: Getting
up, go to the street called
Straight and seek out in the
house of Judas a man of Tarsus,
Saul by name;¹² for behold he is
at prayer and he saw a man
[in a vision], Ananias by name
entering and placing hands upon
him so that he might see again.
¹³ And Ananias answered: Lord,
I heard from many about this
man, what evils he did to your
saints in Jerusalem.¹⁴ And here
he has authority from the high
priests to bind all those
calling upon your name.
¹⁵ And the Lord said to him:
Get going, because he is a
vessel of election of mine
to bear my name before the Gentiles as well as kings and the
sons of Israel. ¹⁶ For I shall
show him how much he must
suffer for the sake of my
name.
¹⁷ And Ananias went away and
entered the house. And when

[12] And a certain Ananias, an up-
right man according to the Law,

he put his hands upon him,
he said: Brother Saul, the
Lord has sent me, Jesus who
appeared to you on the road
on which you were coming, so
that you might see again and
be filled with the Holy Spirit.

18 And immediately something
like scabs fell from his eyes
and he saw again; and when he
got up, he was baptized.
19 And when he took food, he
was strengthened.

20 And straightway, in the
synagogues he was proclaiming
Jesus, that he is the Son of
God. 21 And all who heard were
astonished and were saying:
Is this not the one who made
havoc of those calling upon
this name in Jerusalem and
came here to lead them off
bound to the high priests?
22 And Saul all the more grew
stronger and was confounding
the Jews who were living in

attested to by all the Jewish in-
habitants, ¹³ when he came and ap-
proached me, said: Brother Saul,
see again! And at that hour,
I saw again [at him].
¹⁴ And he said: The God of our
Fathers chose you to know his
will and to see the Just One
and to hear a voice from his
mouth, ¹⁵ because you shall be
a witness on his behalf to all
men concerning what you have
seen and heard. ¹⁶ And now, what
are you waiting for? Get up and
let yourself be baptized and
cleansed of your sins, having
called upon his name.

¹⁹ Wherefore, O King Agrippa, I
have not been disobedient to the
heavenly vision.
²⁰ But I was declaring first to
those in Damascus, then at Jerusalem and the whole country of
Judea, and to the Gentiles that
they should repent and turn to
God, doing works worthy of
repentance.

Damascus, demonstrating that
this one is the Messiah . . .

[17] And it came to pass when I returned to Jerusalem and was praying in the Temple, that I fell into a trance. [18] And I saw him saying to me: Make haste and quickly get out of Jerusalem, because they will not accept your witness concerning me.

[19] And I said: Lord, they understand that from synagogue to synagogue I used to imprison and beat those believing in you. [20] And when the blood of Stephen, your witness, was being shed, I too was present and consenting and guarding the garments of those killing him.

[21] And he said to me: Get going, because I shall send you out far away among the Gentiles. . .

[21] On account of these things, the Jews, seizing me in the Temple, tried to kill me.

[22] Therefore, having attained the help which is from God, up until these days I stand testifying to both small and great, saying nothing apart from what the prophets and Moses said was going to come to pass: [23] that the Messiah is to suffer; that being the first of the resurrection of the dead, he is going to proclaim light both to the people and to the Gentiles. . .

It is quite instructive to compare the three accounts. They evidence several discrepancies which have bothered interpreters ever since the days of the Church Fathers. To begin with, the Ananias episode plays a great role in the first account. But in the second account it is only briefly mentioned, and the complicated double vision is omitted. The third account marks the end of this development—Ananias does not crop up at all, and no mention is made of Paul's being blinded and of his subsequent healing.

In the second account, Paul tells us that soon after his conversion he had a vision of Christ at the temple in Jerusalem. At that time Christ directly told him that he was destined for the Gentile mission: "Depart, for I will send you far away to the Gentiles" (22:21). Neither chapter 9 nor chapter 26 say anything of such a temple vision.

The following feature is even more remarkable. According to chapters 9 and 22, the sole order Paul receives in the vision dialogue outside Damascus is to go into the city. He will learn from Ananias what Christ further intends to do with him. Yet in chapter 26, Christ's command has been changed into a short mission speech (within the vision dialogue) in which the order to undertake the Gentile mission is clearly and unequivocally expressed. Consequently, what Paul learns from Ananias in Damascus (ch. 9) or from Christ himself in a later temple vision (ch 22), he learns directly from Christ before he even comes into the city (ch. 26).

It is also noteworthy that the effect of the heavenly vision upon Paul and his fellow travellers can be told quite differently. According to 9:7, Paul's travelling companions hear the voice but see no one. According to 22:9, they see the light, but this time they cannot hear the voice. Finally, according to 9:7 his companions stand speechless while Paul falls to the ground. But according to 26:14, they all fall down together.

A last point to be noted is the expansion that takes place in the vision dialogue of chapter 26. The address to Paul: "Saul, Saul, why do you persecute me," has another sentence added to it: "It hurts you to kick against the goads" (26:14). This is the first time we hear of such a saying of Christ in the vision dialogue.

2. The Data from the Pauline Letters.

Relative to incidents in the life of the apostle, Paul's letters possess higher value as evidence than does the book of Acts. This point requires no further explanation. Hence it is of great significance that Paul does in fact attest to the Damascus incident in his letters. At this point in his life, God called him through Christ, and this event had deep and long-lasting effects on him. It fed the broader reaches of his theology[16] like an invisible spring. And not seldom it stands unspoken in the background of his thinking, e.g., when he states in the superscription of the letter to the Romans: "Paul, a slave of Jesus Christ, *called to be an apostle,* set apart for the gospel of God . . ." (1:1).[17]

The texts in which Paul *expressly* mentions this incident are 1 Cor 15 and Gal 1,2. We shall consider these texts to see to what extent they agree with the statements of Acts.

1) Agreements between Paul and Acts

(1.) Paul says that he persecuted the Church: "For I am

the least of the apostles, unfit to be called an apostle, because I persecuted the church of God" (1 Cor 15:9). "For you have heard of my former life in Judaism, how I persecuted the church of God violently and tried to destroy it" (Gal 1:13). [18] Perhaps Paul frequently used the phrase: "I persecuted the church," because when he does use it, it sounds like a formula. If we reflect upon the datum that in Acts Christ identifies himself with the Church in the question: "Why do you persecute me?," we can see how closely related the formulas of Acts and the Pauline letters are.

The item that Paul persecuted the Church "violently" (Gal 1:13) also agrees with Acts. His fury is tangibly described[19] in Acts (26:9–11), clearly intimating that Paul was the real dynamo behind the persecution. With his conversion, the whole Church experiences peace (Acts 9:31).

(2.) Paul states most clearly that Christ appeared to him: "Have I not seen Jesus our Lord?" (1 Cor 9:1). "Last of all, as to one untimely born, he appeared also to me" (1 Cor 15:8). With this vision, his persecutory activity came to a sudden and unexpected end. Paul again alludes to this violently sudden change when he says in the letter to the Philippians: "But whatever gain I had, I counted as loss for the sake of Christ" (3:7).

(3.) Paul would exhibit a broader agreement with Acts in 2 Cor 4:6 if this passage does in fact allude to the Damascus incident: "For it is God who said: 'Let light shine out of darkness,' who has shone in our hearts to give the light of the knowledge of the glory of God in the face of Christ."[20] We have already indicated the significance ascribed to *light* precisely in the Lukan Damascus accounts. And Acts 22:11 specifically mentions the *doxa,* the brilliance emanating from Christ. However, there is no clear proof to indicate that Paul's vocation vision does in fact stand behind what he says in 2 Cor 4:6.[21]

(4.) Paul considers the vision in which God revealed his Son to him (Gal 1:16) as intimately connected with his call to be apostle of the Gentiles. For the Son was revealed to him *so that* he might proclaim him among the Gentiles (Gal 1:16). Here too there is agreement with Acts. At least in chapter 26, the call to the Gentile mission immediately follows the self-revelation of Christ (v. 16).

(5.) Finally, Paul, like Acts, connects the whole incident with Damascus. This is indirectly apparent from the statement in Gal 1:17: ". . . and again I returned to Damascus."[22] However, this indirect testimony does not allow us to determine whether the vision took place *in* or *outside of* Damascus.

Thus on a number of fundamental points, the Pauline letters confirm the description of the event in Acts. This is especially significant because it cannot be proved that Luke—or better, the author of Acts—knew the Pauline letters. Hence what Acts say about Paul's conversion is based upon relatively independent traditions of Syrian and Palestinian Christian communities which at an early date told of the unexpected conversion of the persecutor. What Paul says in Gal 1:22–24 is instructive on this point: "And I was still not known by sight to the churches of Christ in Judea; they only heard it said: 'He who once persecuted us is now preaching the faith he once tried to destroy.' And they glorified God because of me." This statement presupposes that the news of Paul's conversion reached the Christian communities of Judea and Jerusalem independently of Paul. That details about this conversion were told in the process of spreading the news is not excluded by Gal 1:22–24, but rather suggested by it: praise to God followed upon the news of the persecutor's conversion.[23]

Where the Pauline letters and Acts confirm each other, we

have reliable historical traditions. But there are differences between Paul and Luke. We now turn to these differences.

2) Disagreements between Paul and Acts

(1.) It is remarkable that in his letters Paul does not *narrate* his vocation at all like he does in Acts 22 and 26. Although the event was the turning point of his life, yet he mentions it only in a very few passages, and even in these he does so "in all brevity—and in passing."[24] However, one can argue that this is due to the quite different types of writing involved; in Acts the incident has to be narrated, while in a letter Paul needs only to allude to what he had already told his addressees earlier.[25] But does this in fact explain Paul's terseness on the subject of his vocation vision? Specifically in the case of the Galatians, among whom his apostolic status was called into doubt, it would have been more sensible to apeak at length about what his call entailed. Yet Paul in fact mentions that incident only in a subordinate clause (Gal 1:15). This scarcity of information seems to derive from Paul's personal, deep reserve. Re-read 2 Cor 12:1-4, for example, to see how Paul expresses himself concerning his "visions and revelations." He mentions the subject only in self-defense; and he changes into the third person ("I know of a man . . ."); then he abruptly breaks off in v. 5. It would seem that he found it unpleasant to speak of such things.

Now this leads us to the question as to whether Paul ever told anyone of his call in the way he is said to in Acts 22 and 26. He certainly often emphatically stressed that "I have seen the Lord," and that not only in 1 Cor 9:1.

But aside from this, did he ever report any details?

(2.) Paul's "I have seen the Lord" points to another discrepancy. As unequivocal as this Pauline statement sounds, according to Acts it would seem that Paul never saw the Lord at all. Acts states that Paul was flooded by a heavenly light; and from this one gets the impression that he, like Moses before the burning bush, saw only a vision of light, and not the shape or form of Christ. But is this impression correct? When the text states that Paul's companions saw "no one," this seemingly implies that *Paul* surely saw "some one." Besides, Ananias says: "The God of our fathers appointed you . . . *to see the Just One* and to hear a voice from his mouth" (22:14). And similar statements are to be found in 9:17,27 and 26:16. To this day exegetes are divided on the interpretation of this matter in Acts. [26]

The fundamental question is: what does Luke really intend to say? That Paul saw the Lord himself is rather obvious for Luke. Even a statement like Acts 22:14 shows this. Yet at the same time, he clearly avoids stating something like this directly in his report of the vision. For example, Luke reports Paul saying before Agrippa and Festus: ". . . I saw on the way a light from heaven, brighter than the sun, shining round me and those who journeyed with me" (Acts 26:13). But Paul does not continue—and this is the point: ". . . and in this light *I saw someone* who said to me . . ." Rather Paul states that he heard a voice speaking. The indirectness of this report is clear. Luke, therefore, leaves the question as to *how* Paul actually saw Christ quite consciously undecided. And if he does intend to leave his description open-ended and blurry, we certainly ought not attempt to do away with this blurriness. [27]

We might learn why Luke describes Paul's vision the way he does by looking at the way he describes the Easter appearances of Christ in chapter 24 of his gospel and in chapter 1 of Acts. In the context of the Easter appearances, it is simply unthinkable for him to say of the apostles: "They saw a light and heard a voice."[28] There is no mention at all of a light emanating from shining about the figure of Christ. Rather the apostles respond quite directly to the risen Jesus. They even eat and drink with him.[29] The apparition character of these encounters is intimated only through Christ's manner of coming and vanishing.[30] The description of the risen Jesus here, which so sharply contrasts with that of the Damascus incident, corresponds well with the fact that according to Luke, the Resurrection appearances last only 40 days and come to a close with the Ascension of Christ. In this perspective, the Ascension forms a solid line of demarcation in Luke's two volume work.[31] And the conclusion is obvious: *for Luke the appearance of Christ outside Damascus simply does not belong to the Easter appearances of Jesus.* By leaving what Paul actually saw undecided—was it only a shining light or a figure in this light—Luke reveals one of his methods of contrasting the vision outside Damascus with the Easter appearances of the 40 day period.[32]

These observations already somewhat anticipate what will be treated in detail in the third part of this work, i.e., the literary and theological activity of Luke. But these anticipated considerations are necessary to highlight an even more striking difference between Luke and Paul. For what proves right for Paul is precisely the opposite of what Luke intimates. For Paul the Damascus vision does in fact belong to the series of Easter appearances of Jesus. This follows clearly from the important text, 1 Cor 15:3-9:

For I delivered to you as of first importance what I also received, that Christ died for our sins in accordance with the scriptures, that he was buried, that he was raised on the third day in accordance with the scriptures, and that he appeared to Cephas, then to the twelve.

Then he appeared to more than five-hundred brethren at one time, most of whom are still alive, though some have fallen asleep. Then he appeared to James, then to all the apostles. Last of all, as to one untimely born, he appeared also to me. For I am the least of the apostles, unfit to be called an apostle, because I persecuted the church of God.

Here Paul gives the Corinthians testimony which serves as proof for the Resurrection of Christ. And he follows the fixed tradition of the primitive Church, at least in the statements beginning with "that." Now it is important that he lists himself among the witnesses to the resurrection; and in this he presupposes that the appearance accorded him is quite similar to those he previously enumerates.[33] The only point of difference he sees in it all is that he was unworthy of his call.

That Paul holds a view of the matter which is actually quite different from Luke's can be seen again by a look at Acts. Acts 13:31-33 offers an interesting text for comparison with 1 Cor 15:3-9. This passage also talks of the Resurrection of Christ; it too introduces witnesses as proof; and what is more significant, Paul is speaking. The context is a long speech made by Paul in the synagogue at Antioch (in Pisidia) Paul says: "But God raised him from the dead; and for many days he appeared to those who came up with him from Galilee to Jerusalem, who are now his witnesses to the people. And we bring you the good news that what God promised to the fathers, this he has fulfilled to us their children by raising Jesus."

The attentive reader will take note of the subtle nuance in the text: ". . . who are now his witnesses . . . And *we* bring you the good news . . ." The distinction between "them" and "us" means that Paul and Barnabas simply do not belong to the circle of witnesses proper. The passage likewise stands in opposition to the Pauline letters in that in this report, it does not at all occur to Paul to recall his own commissioning by the resurrected Jesus. Rather he bases his preaching *solely* and exclusively on the authority of those witnesses who followed Jesus from Galilee onwards. Did Paul actually speak in this way?[34]

(3.) Now we come to another difference between Paul and Acts which is closely connected to what has been said thus far. Paul understood himself to be an apostle on the basis of the call he received outside Damascus. "Am I not an apostle? Have I not seen Jesus our Lord?" (1 Cor 9:1). Whoever would assail him on this score would touch the deepest roots of his self-understanding. This is shown especially in his letter to the Corinthians.

Thus, it is all the more astounding that Paul, according to the perspective of Acts, is simply not an apostle. Luke reserves this designation for the Twelve.[35] To be sure, in Acts 14:4,14 Paul is called an apostle together with Barnabas, but here Luke takes the word in an unspecific sense (i.e., from the viewpoint of his theology).[36] Von Campenhausen correctly states: "If one considers . . . how often Luke would have had occasion to highlight Paul in emphatic and solemn fashion and yet does not do so, then one will not introduce this solitary passage against the unequivocal total evidence."[37]

For Luke, the only persons who are in fact apostles are those who accompanied Jesus from the beginning of his public ministry in Galilee to Jerusalem, who witnessed the Easter appearances of Jesus within the 40 day period, and above all, whom Jesus himself chose to be apostles. These characteristics are programmatically described in Acts 1:21–26 (the selection of Matthias).[38] This passage makes it evident that Luke considers the apostles as the proper vehicles of the continuity between the time of the earthly Jesus and the time of the Church. Paul, on the other hand, has an entirely different function for Luke. As the great missionary to the Gentiles, he is the connecting link between the apostolically stamped time of the Church's beginnings and the time of Luke himself. The Lukan idea of an apostle which is so strongly defined by the relationship to the earthly Jesus, has no room for Paul as an apostle.

(4.) Though Paul does not deny his connections to the traditions of the primitive Church,[39] yet he is convinced that he received his call and his gospel *directly* from God: "Paul, an apostle—not from men nor through man—but through Jesus Christ and God the Father." Thus begins the letter to the Galatians. And Gal 1:11,12 has: "For I would have you know, brethren, that the gospel which was preached by me is not man's gospel. For I did not receive it from man, nor was I taught it, but it came through a revelation of Jesus Christ."

Does this passage indicate a final difference between Luke and Paul on the nature of an apostle? For at least according to chapters 9 and 22 of Acts, Paul at first receives no revelation which tells him what to do; he finally does learn what God has planned for him only through Ananias. H. Conzelmann interprets the data of Acts thus: "Differently than in Gal 1:12f., Paul does not learn the gospel in the vision itself; he is referred to the Church as mediatrix of doctrine."[40] G. Klein states this view even more forcibly: in Acts the conversion and call of Paul are not identical. As a representative of the Church, Ananias plays the decisive mediatory role for Paul. In this way, he receives his legitimation only by his being inserted into the tradition of the Church, and he is deprived of any basis enabling him to understand his call and office as coming directly from God.[41] We shall later decide whether the interpretation of Conzelmann and Klein are correct or not. For the time being, we should just like to note that on this matter, too, Luke holds a point of view entirely different from Paul's.

All the aforementioned differences between Acts and the Pauline letters naturally lead to the question whether the author of Acts was really a fellow worker and sometime companion of Paul. The scope envisioned by this study is too narrow for a critical examination of this intricate question, which in fact is the subject of sharp discussion nowadays (E. Haenchen, H. Conzelmann, G. Klein). Yet from all that has been said, it should be apparent that it is rather impossible to presuppose simply that Luke had been directly informed about the Damascus vision by Paul himself.

II.

Two Older Methods
of
Interpretation

We have just given a broad survey of the New Testament material dealing with the call and conversion of Paul. And we have seen that this material contains similarities as well as dissimilarities and blatant discords. These dissimilarities and discordant elements have, of course, been often noted in the past. By and large, how have interpreters dealt with these disagreements in the texts?

1. The Conservative Way.

Commentators have often noted that Luke himself explains, in the preface to his first book, that he had "followed all things closely" and written "an orderly account" of the "things which have been accomplished among us" (Luke 1:1-4).[42] Now Luke certainly did not change these principles which guided his work when he authored his second book, the Acts. Consequently every detail of the three conversion accounts in Acts must be taken seriously as "historical fact." Hence, to reconstruct what factually took place outside Damascus, one would only have to tally up the data presented in the three accounts of Acts and in the statements of Paul's letters. This opinion was, more or less, commonly held by all Catholic biblical interpreters almost up to the middle of this century.[43] Thus A. Steinmann, whose commentary on Acts appeared in the *Bonner Bibel* (4th edition, 1934), wrote on our subject: "Accordingly, the correct assessment of the aforementioned discrepancies among the three accounts is this: the individual items are not mutually contradictory, but rather they proffer, if we add them up, a more or less full picture of everything that took place at the conversion" (p. 91).

At times, some authors even maintained that the disagreements in the texts would be proof that these passages are accounts deriving from genuine witnesses. Thus A. Bisping, in his series of commentaries on the New Testament (1866) wrote: "In substance, all three accounts agree exactly; yet they do differ from each other in non-essentials. But because of this, their credibility is not diminished; rather the historical character of the presentation is thus guaranteed" (p. 157). And even in 1957, W. Prokulski stated: "Today critics do not attach much importance to these discrepancies. They see in them, in fact, a proof of the authenticity of the story, for a complete uniformity in the accounts, they argue, would suggest that these had been prepared beforehand *ad hoc*."[44] Prokulski's assessment of the tendency of interpretation after World War II is highly one-sided. He is correct in that the discrepancies are no longer accorded great importance today, but certainly not because they are considered to be the common, natural imprecisions of eye-witness reports. Rather these disagreements are explained by the literary style of the author and by the literary conventions he used.[45] Nevertheless, Prokulski's viewpoint excellently reflects the tendency of the older, conservative way of biblical interpretation.

An obvious example of this older direction of interpretation is offered by J. Knabenbauer, in the *Cursus Scripturae Sacrae*.[46] In his view, the first account in Acts 9 contains the most precise and thorough description of the whole incident. For it is historically much more probable ("e rei veritate convenit") that with Paul lying on the ground, Christ gave him just the short command to enter the city rather than the detailed instructions of chapter 26. The small differences in the two other accounts ought not be explained by means of various sources. Paul was Luke's sole source since Luke was Paul's companion.[47] Likewise, the two speeches in chapters 22 and 26 are a historical report of what Paul actually said at the time when he addressed the Jews and King Agrippa respectively. The two discrepancies in Acts 26 (the whole Ananias episode is lacking; in its place Christ gives a previously unmentioned mission charge to Paul) are explained as due to the description which Paul himself gave. This description was conditioned by the presence of the royal audience; for, in these circumstances, Paul chose to combine what in reality took place in different situations and at different times.[48]

Those who advocate the line of interpretation illustrated here with Knabenbauer always stress that the direct source of the accounts of Acts is Paul himself. We offer a sampling of this point of view: J.M. Voste: Luke had composed what his teacher Paul reported to him.[49] A. Steinmann: The conversion would have been "a favorite topic of conversation between the apostle and his disciple."[50] E. Meyer: Luke would have heard the account of the conversion often enough from the mouth of Paul; Paul must "have told (of the Damascus vision) countless times."[51]

While the principle stays the same, there is naturally a difference of opinion among conservative exegetes over specifics. Thus Foakes-Jackson[52] traces back all the discrepancies in the Lukan description to narrative variants deriving from Paul. "As a companion of Paul he must often have been told the story. But the accounts of such an experience are bound to vary in detail when related at different times, and the Apostle may well have had a confused recollection as to the less important details of so tremendous a spiritual experience" (p. 80).

D. M. Stanley[53] explains the disagreements somewhat differently. He is so struck by the similarities of the accounts in chapters 9 and 22 that he concludes as follows: the Pauline speech which Luke sets down in chapter 22 must have formed the main source for the narrative in chapter 9. The concrete details described in chapter 9 "point to the possibility that there was a second source—perhaps Ananias."

P. Gaechter[54] envisions the problem differently again. He explains "the parallel reports about the events connected with the vision (Acts 9:10-19; 22:12-16)" by appealing to the different ways in which they were shaped and elaborated by tradition.[55] The peculiarity of the third account (Acts 26:16b-18) is not due to the specific concrete circumstances of Paul's speaking before King Agrippa. Rather, the third account reveals how Paul himself later theologically interpreted the Damascus event. For Paul the historical course of events gets crowded up (Gaechter speaks of a telescoping of events); and he now interprets the event in terms of Old Testament passages like Jer 1:5-8 and Is 49:1. It is only when he comes to describing the vision itself that things are different. Here Gaechter states with great certainty: "Insofar as the actual vision is involved, all three accounts mutually agree. The narrative is entirely straightforward and without psychological and theological interpretation; and therefore it may be judged to be the original account of the Apostle."[56]

However, let us turn for a moment to but one concrete problem, namely the fact that the effect of the vision of Christ upon Paul and his companions is described so differently in the three accounts. A whole arsenal of attempts has been marshalled to explain this feature. And these attempts show to what extent this line of interpretation—insisting on its presupposition that each detail is historical-leads to embarassment because of Luke's literary style of composing. Let us recall that in the first account (9:7) the companions hear the voice; in the second account (22:9), they do not hear the voice.

From the time of Chrysostom[57] till our own day, some have continually held that the "voice" of Acts 9:7 does not refer to the voice of Christ, but to the voice of Paul.[58] Thus more recently, F. F. Bruce states in his much reprinted commentary: " . . . 'the voice' *(tes phones)* here refers to *Paul's* voice; his companions heard him speaking, but saw no one to whom the speaking could be addressed."[59] But this explanation is thoroughly wrecked by v. 4 ("he heard *a voice*"), to which v. 7 refers. Besides, as the parallel accounts show, what Luke specifically intends to express here is that to a certain degree Paul's companions can share in the miraculous vision.

There is another solution which is put forward much more frequently. In the Greek text, both passages have the same word for "voice" *(phone)*. Different meanings of the word are then distinguished in good scholastic fashion. Depending on context, the word could signify either an *articulate* voice or an *inarticulate* one. Chapter 9 states that they. heard the voice—hence an inarticulate voice would be meant. On the other hand, chapter 22 states that they did not hear the voice—that would mean that only Paul understood the words of the voice.[60] T. Zahn[61] stated this view most plainly: (The companions of Paul) *saw* the lightning-like light illuminating the area around them, but no human form as the source of the light rays. They also *heard* a thunder-like voice, but they did not understand what it called out and to whom it was addressed." This attempted solution is, at bottom, a possible one, for we do in fact have reports from antiquity in which those present at a vision hear something but cannot understand what is being said. Thus John 12:28,29 tells of a heavenly voice which addresses Jesus: "I have glorified it, and I will glorify it again"; but the by-standers think it thundered. Be that as it may, the question here is whether *our* text may be understood in this way. The fact is that because of the definite article before the word "voice" *(phone)* in the statement of v. 7 ("they heard *the voice"),* the sentence refers back to v. 4. And that verse mentions only an *articulate* voice. Besides, how would the reader get to know anything at all about an inarticulate voice in chapter 9?[62]

Finally, let us note Prokulski's fanciful solution: "When Paul came to his senses, he told his companions what had happened to him, and some of them then thought that they had seen the light and others that they had heard the voices. This would explain the discrepancies between the different accounts."[63]

The reaction of Paul's companions in this scene—they either fall down or stay standing—makes for even greater difficulties for conservative exegesis. For the first account does in fact state: "The men who were traveling with him stood speechless . . . " (9:7), while the third account states: "And when we had all fallen to the ground . . . " (26:14). But dauntless exegetes will never be nonplussed. Thus, A. Bisping: "The contradiction is easily solved by the supposition that the companions of Saul first fell down with him, but immediately got up again and then stood there speechless, while Saul, upon whom the whole impression worked more forcefully, lay upon the ground, stunned."[64]

A. Steinmann[65] allows the choice of another possibility: "There can be talk of an irreconcilable contradiction only if the data of one (account) exclude the data of the other. That is not the case. Rather one ought imagine that upon Paul's falling down and their experiencing the effects of the peculiar light, the traveling companions of Paul are astounded and come to a halt; subsequently they are overcome by the unusual apparition and fall to the ground . . . *or* that all fall down together, but unlike Paul, his companions get up and look on at the way things develop in perplexed surprise. When helpful hands assisted the blinded Paul to his feet, he concluded that his companions must have gotten up".

Finally—and in spite of Acts 26:14:—there were some who did not hesitate to explain the texts as follows: depending on how far they stood from where the vision took place, one group of Paul's companions would have remained standing, while the other would have fallen to the ground.[66]

There is a more widespread explanation that perhaps ought be taken more seriously. According to this view, the Greek verb in 9:7 translated, "they stood" *(heistekeisan)*, really does not have this meaning, but should rather be translated in a more attenuated way with "they were."[67] Yet what moves some authors to this translation are purely and emphatically apologetic reasons. For without knowledge of the problems raised by 26:14, no one would ever have thought of translating *heistekeisan* in this way. Given the circumstance of Paul lying on the ground (cf. 9:4,6), the Greek *heistekeisan eneoi* simply means: "they stood speechless."

These last few examples clearly show that with such methods of interpretation one has the basis for eliminating every discordant element in the Bible. Note the ready and constant reference to psychology and psychologizing. Paul's companions quickly spring up from the ground; first they stand back full of astonishment, then the appraition begins to work on them; those standing farther down the road are not affected by the apparition. What really is in the text about all this? Furthermore, note that the differences between Acts and the Pauline letters mentioned above are hardly ever considered to be a problem. This point too is not surprising. For is it is held to be certain that the author of Acts was a companion of Paul, and that the speeches of Paul in Acts are trustworthy reports of what Paul actually said, then there can be no fundamental differences at all between Paul's letters and Acts.

Be that as it may, I believe enough has already been said about the method of interpretation which I have summarily named "the conservative way." Its weaknesses and imbalanced one-sidedness are obvious. Nevertheless this method has in fact produced much worthwhile material in the area of word study and detailed historical background for the explanation of the text. And its basic perspective and thrust—that we must take the vision outside Damascus seriously as an actual and real incident—was and remains correct. For it is with this perspective that the aforecited exegetes were concerned, even if they championed that goal with inadequate means.

2. The Attempted Solutions of Literary Criticism.

Literary criticism attempted to deal with the differences among the three accounts from an entirely different frame of reference. But what is "literary criticism" all about anyway?

In biblical studies, the term "literary criticism" is normally used synonymously with *source analysis.* The literary critical method is employed to investigate contradictions and discrepancies in the text. With the help of these literary irregularities, the method attempts to sort out the possible *sources* utilized by a given author or editor which were not neatly absorbed into his work. The terminology of the method includes items such as literary irregularities, catchwords, literary seams, summaries, style changes, doublets, editorial insertions, glosses, interpolations, and the like. Literary criticism saw its heyday in the 19th century; in that period its scalpel was applied to nearly all the famous works of world literature, be it Shakespeare or Homer, the Nibelungenlied or the Gilgamesh epic. Naturally literary criticism did not pull up to a stop before the texts of the Bible.

The literary critical method is actually of greater importance for understanding works in which various sources or previous compositions have been worked in than it is for original, independent works. And since the texts of the Old Testament as well as the New are frequently the products of previous sources or compositions, the literary critical method simply cannot be kept away from scientific biblical exegesis. The classical example of literary criticism in the Old Testament is the so-called Pentateuchal criticism which has uncovered several originally distinct sources in the first books of the Bible: the Yahwistic source (J [called "J" because in German the tetragrammaton is spelled "Jahwe"]), the Elohistic source (E), the Priestly document (P).[68]

In the area of the New Testament, the so-called *Synoptic question,* i.e., the question of the mutual relationship of the first three gospels, is solved in literary cricical fashion by most exegetes; Mark's gospel is presumed to be a source document for both Matthew and Luke. In addition, Matthew and Luke make use of a common source consisting of sayings of Jesus (Logia); this source is referred to by the abbreviation "Q" (German "Quelle" means "source"). To a certain extent literary criticism can infer the existence of common discourse material in Matthew and Luke; yet no *direct* dependence between Matthew and Luke can be proved. Hence scholars have concluded that two principal sources account for all three gospels, namely Mark and Q. This *Two-Source Theory* has easily and satisfactorily solved many Synoptic problems and has done so—and this is most significant—in a purely literary way.[69]

The literary critical viewpoint naturally suggested that the repetition of the Damascus vision in Acts 22 and 26 as well as the differences in the three accounts derive from different sources. Luke would have had different sources dealing with Paul's conversion at his disposal. The main analyses of the conversion accounts in this frame of reference were carried out by F. Spitta in 1891,[70] J. Jüngst in 1895,[71] H. H. Wendt in 1913,[72] E. Hirsch in 1929,[73] K. Lake in 1933,[74] and E. Trocmé in 1957.[75]

Of these authors, Spitta, Jüngst, Hirsch, and Trocmé carry literary criticism to the extreme, i.e., they claim they can tell us precisely from which source each verse derives. For Spitta and Jüngst, the editor of Acts limited himself to interweaving his sources in very subtle fashion.

On the other hand, Wendt, Lake and Trocmé conclude that the author of the work greatly reworked his sources. It would be superfluous to sketch the results of these investigations in detail here. But to appreciate the method, we offer a consideration of the sources distinguised by Hirsch, since his literary critical analysis of the Damascus story is quite distinct and exemplary.

To begin with, Hirsch saw that the first and third accounts deviate from each other most strongly, while chapter 22 holds an in-between position. The Ananias episode illustrates this very well; it plays a great role in chapter 9, it is shortened in chapter 22, and it is entirely lacking in chapter 26. Hirsch further observed, with many an author before him, that the third account of Acts most greatly agrees with the statements of the Pauline letters. Recall that Paul does not speak of Ananias in his letters; rather he stresses that he received his revelation without intermediary. The vision of Christ meant for him his call to be apostle of the Gentiles. Now it is precisely all these points that correspond with Acts 26. On the contrary, notes Hirsch, there is actually no mention of a call to be apostle of the Gentiles in chapter 9. "A persecutor of Christians is cast down through Jesus; he is then accorded the Spirit and baptism within the Christian community—this is the whole content of the narrative" (307). Thus the first and third accounts are mutually exclusive.

Given these data, the following conclusions may be drawn. In chapter 26 we possess extremely reliable historical tradition; because of the close relationship of this chapter with the Pauline letters, we can say that we clearly have Paul's own account. More specifically, this means that "the way in which Paul himself spoke of his conversion underlies (the third account)" (309). Chapter 9, on the contrary, goes back to another source of a more legendary nature. And this source must derive from the Christian community in Damascus because it specifies the name of the street where Paul lived in that city as well as his host's name (cf. 9:11), and it describes an appearance of Jesus to a member of that community. Paul's conversion was spoken of in Damascus much like in chapter 9. There the whole incident was considered "as a strict judgment on Paul" which preserved the community from imminent persecution (307).

Luke reproduced both the Damascus tradition as well as the Pauline conception of the incident "with straight-forward fidelity" (309). In chapter 22, however, "he reveals to us how he conceived the two accounts could be brought into agreement" (309f.). He based himself upon the first account but rightly bent it in the direction of the Pauline tradition. Therefore, the second account is a "mixed form" constructed from chapters 9 and 26 (308).

As one can see, the literary critical solution, here exemplified by the work of Hirsch, significantly differs from the method of "conservative" interpreters. The latter strived to harmonize divergencies in the text as much as possible and sought to view the three accounts in terms of an inner unity. Literary criticism, however, does just the opposite; it delves into the differences in the text and strives specifically to elaborate and distinguish the various forms of chapters 9 and 26. Once the antithetical structure of the texts is recognized and traced back to two different sources, literary critics feel that all the differences among the three accounts can be solved without difficulty. Consequently, to get back to Hirsch, *in the Pauline tradition,* all of Paul's companions saw the light and fell down. And this agrees with the factual, historical course of events (311). On the other hand, *according to the Damascus tradition,* Paul's fellow travelers heard a voice, but saw no light. Thus the matter is quite understandable! For the Damascus tradition did in fact insert the legendary motif of the blinding of Paul (311f.). Hence in that tradition the companions should not see the light; otherwise, they also would have been blinded (310).

Generally speaking, it cannot be denied that Hirsch's solution is neat and well worked out. It does seem convincing. Not only does it account for the differences within Acts, but it also answers the disagreements between Acts and the Pauline letters. These discrepancies can now be explained quite extensively and solved easily and convincingly with the help of the two different sources.

Yet the solution's neatness and convincing quality still do not prove its correctness. Haenchen has rightly objected to it, and for the following reason. According to Hirsch's hypothesis, Luke is basically a modern historian, possessing two notable sources. He does not wish to pass over either source, but does inform his readers about how he himself would reconstruct the incident behind both sources. The difficulty with this view is that Luke in reality is an early Christian edificatory author. He does not reveal the least interest in informing his readers about variations in the tradition.[76] In other words, Hirsch's conception of the author of Acts is rather anachronistic.

Moreover, there is a second objection to Hirsch's view that is much more serious.[77] Hirsch maintained that the third account of Acts simply excludes the first account (307). But there are very few who agree with him. In fact the first account already hints at Paul's commission to the Gentiles (cf. 9:15). And in no way does the first account intimate "strict judgment" on Paul.[78]

But perhaps the absence of the Ananias episode in the third account indicates that another tradition underlies the account. Does it? To focus upon this feature is to shift the discussion about the specifics of Hirsch's views to a point that continually claims the attention of nearly all source analysts of the Damascus story. For Wendt, Lake and Trocmé do in fact base their attempts to separate sources in Acts on the absence of the Ananias episode and the *direct* commissioning of Paul to the Gentile mission in chapter 26.[79]

Yet in face of this, the peculiarity of the third account can be explained much more simply in terms of *Luke's literary craft.* In the third account, he simply *summarizes* and *abridges* what he treated of twice previously. If we give him credit for a sufficient amount of literary creativity in this respect, then we need not look to special sources to explain the varied structures of the accounts. In fact, the majority of interpreters have always inclined in this direction, and the ascription of the Damascus accounts to different sources never really carried the day.[80] Yet it is only *today's* interpreters of the Damascus story who feel the greatest reluctance and show the least readiness to work with separate sources.[81] The reason for this is that the intense research into Acts over the last few years has yielded the growing insight that we are dealing with an *"author"* in Acts. In other words, the interpreter of Acts must be ever aware of the literary art and compositional techniques of the author, Luke.[82] This point brings us to the real subject matter of this book, namely *the methods of contemporary exegesis.* Our purpose is to demonstrate this method. But this simultaneously entails describing the literary creativity with which Luke authored his material. Thus, in the remainder of this book it will become demonstrably clear why neither the conservative way nor the literary critical method can really solve the problems related to the Damascus story.

Two concluding remarks are still in order here. To begin with, we believe that literary criticism does not offer a convincing solution to the Damascus story. But we do believe that in many other cases of biblical interpretation, this method is in fact extremely useful and necessary.

Furthermore, while we reject the idea of distinct sources for the Damascus accounts, we do not exclude the possibility that individual traditional items of various origin were contained in the material Luke had about Paul's conversion. For example, the vision in the Jerusalem temple (Acts 22:17-21) could derive from such an individual tradition.[83] We are sceptical only as to whether traditions of this sort, which could be simply single items of information, can in fact be extracted en bloc from the Lukan composition like classical literary criticism has attempted to do. And we are equally sceptical about the possibility of tracing back the differences among the accounts to different traditions.[84]

III.

The Method
of
Contemporary Exegesis

With our objections to the literary critical solution at the close of the last chapter, we have already pointed to the direction that contemporary exegesis takes. Modern scholarship has gradually learned that the speeches of the New Testament are not some type of tape recording transcripts, and that New Testament reports and narratives were not meant to be scripts for documentary films of the events they portray. The primitive Christian Church would have been in no position to produce the type of documentation that is normative in modern historical science. And most of all, the early Chruch would have shown no interest in anything of the sort.

Contemporary exegesis has also learned that New Testament authors should not be imagined simply as mechanical compilers of written sources and community traditions. They were in fact authors. For example, the theological conviction of the individual evangelists is clearly and sharply reflected in the way they have collected their traditional material, in the way they have combined and organized that material, and in the way they have somewhat reshaped it. But our intention is not to theorize, but to demonstrate with the text of Acts how present-day exegesis proceeds!

1. The Speeches of Acts.

Two of the three accounts of Paul's conversion and call are situated in speeches. Were these speeches delivered at that time in the form in which we have them? "Conservative" interpreters would naturally say "yes" to the question; for Acts is a work of history, and in such a work nothing ought to be made up! This latter presupposition undergirds the whole modern understanding of historical science. Ancient authors, too, respected the demand for historical truth.[85] But the question is whether their conception of historical truth covers the same ground that ours does. To answer this question, we should sample the various literary forms they used to express historical truth in antiquity. Now among these literary forms, the *speech* shows quite specifically how authors of antiquity could at least express historical truth in *forms* like our own, but in an entirely different manner.

For example, in the Hellenistic period literary taste dictated that an author should break up his rather monotone work be inserting speeches at various intervals.[86] By following this literary convention, the Hellenistic author surely did not think he was relating the exact and precise words of speeches that were actually given, and neither did his readers. To insert a speech in his work, the author did not need to find out whether a speech had been made at all. Indeed, we can even show that ancient historians did not relate the text of a speech they actually knew or heard delivered, but rather composed entirely new ones that better suited their own taste and more adequately fitted the literary conventions and style governing their work. Thus in his *Annals* (XI, 24) Tacitus transmits the speech of Emperor Claudius concerning the bestowal of the *ius honorum* upon the Gauls and delivered before the Roman senate. Now we do in fact have the original wording of this particular speech from an inscription,[87] and it differs markedly from what Tacitus offers in the *Annals*, although he certainly must have known the text of the original speech.[88]

The first-century Jewish historian, Flavius Josephus, reveals some very instructive literary techniques in his *Jewish Antiq-*

uities. As is well known, Josephus follows the Old Testament text in the first books of his work. And he is convinced that the books of Moses, the Pentateuch, are historically reliable. In fact he praises Moses for eschewing all lies and idle fables.[89] Yet the freedom with which he reproduces these books is rather astonishing. This aspect is especially apparent in the narrative of the sacrifice of Isaac. Genesis 22:7-10 runs:

> So they went both of them together. And Isaac said to his father Abraham, "My father!" And he said, "Here am I, my son." He said "Behold the fire and the wood; but where is the lamb for a burnt offering?" Abraham said, "God will provide himself the lamb for a burnt offering, my son." So they went both of them together. When they came to the place of which God had told him, Abraham built an altar there, and laid the wood in order, and bound Isaac his son, and laid him on the altar, upon the wood. Then Abraham put forth his hand, and took the knife to slay his son.[90]

Thus according to the Genesis account, the last words exchanged between Isaac and his father are spoken on the way to the mountain. The text then continues telling how Abraham prepares the sacrifice *without a word* spoken until the angel of Yahweh calls down from heaven. Josephus reports the story quite differently. In his account, after Abraham has everything ready for the sacrifice, he stops to make a speech to his son, as follows:

> My child, myriad were the prayers in which I besought God for thy birth, and when thou camest into the world, no pains were there that I did not lavish upon thine upbringing, no thought had I of higher happiness than

to see thee grown to man's estate and to leave thee at
my death heir to my dominion. But, since it was by
God's will that I became thy sire and now again as
pleases Him I am resigning thee, bear thou this con-
secration valiantly; for it is to God I yield thee, to
God who now claims from us this homage in return
for the gracious favor He has shown me as my sup-
porter and ally. Aye, since thou wast born out of the
course of nature, so quit thou now this life not by
the common road, but sped by thine own father on the
way to God the Father of all, through the rites of
sacrifice. He accounts it not meet for thee to depart
this life by sickness or war or by any of the calamities
that commonly befall mankind, but amid prayers and
sacrificial ceremonies would receive thy soul and keep it
near to Himself; and for me thou shalt be a protector
and stay of my old age—to which end above all I
nurtured thee—by giving me God in the stead of thyself.[91]

Here we need not go into the disappointing superficiality
and caricature of history that Josephus achieves with this
monologue. What interests us only is that this ancient historian puts a speech in Abraham's mouth, and the .Genesis text
offers no point of contact for this speech. Josephus apparently considers this procedure legitimate. And he certainly does
not think his inserting the speech contradicts what he said
in his extensive prologue, where he stressed that he would
write "neither adding nor omitting anything," but simply
set forth "the precise details of our Scripture records."[92]
The example of Josephus shows how differently an ancient
author, specifically a Hellenistic historian, viewed his task.
For him a narrative took on life and color only by the use
of speeches composed according to literary convention. By
putting speeches into the mouths of important personages of

an episode, he gains a welcome means of being able to *clarify* and *interpret* a given personality, situation, or the course of an event. Modern historians generally try to distinguish what their sources say from their own interpretation of those sources, and this as exactly as possible. The ancient historian, on the contrary, weaves both his sources and his own interpretation of the sources into a literary unity.

Consequently, if we choose to read ancient historical texts through the sharp lens of modern historiography, and then raise the question of historical truth in terms of our modern perspective of the matter, we certainly ought not to ask whether the speech in question actually took place exactly or at least in much the same way as reported or not. Rather our question must be: does the interpretation of the facts presented in this speech agree with the facts themselves? Has the historical reality been interpreted correctly?

Thus the speeches contained in ancient historical documents are *a medium of free and creative literary compositional expression.* And the same would apply, generally speaking, to the speeches of Acts (with certain reservations). The following observations should point this up more specifically.[93]

1.) The book of Acts contains an extraordinary number of speeches. According to Dibelius,[94] there are some 24 such speeches, that is a fourth to a fifth of the whole book! This figure excludes shorter addresses and statements like, e.g., 6:2-4; 8:20-23; 9:15,16; 21:20-25, since they do not bear a discernible speech style. Without all these speeches, Acts would look like a truncated torso, and certainly not like the work we known as the book of Acts. This feature, therefore, indicates that for Luke, the speeches form one of the most important stylistic divices in his second book. And specifically because these speeches are such an intensively applied *stylistic device,* we are led to ask whether they were actually delivered in the way we have them.

2.) The speeches in Acts are just about evenly distributed over the entire book; and this too is an important observation.[95] Further, if one grants that the sources for the individual parts of Acts must have been very diverse, then it seems quite clear that the speeches of Acts are in fact a literary, stylistic device employed by Luke. The reason for this is that although there is great diversity of source materials for the individual sections of the book, the consistency of speeches is rather stable throughout Acts. Hence the author must be responsible for the consistency.

3.) The speeches are all too brief. If they were really delivered in the form that we have them, then most of them would have lasted no more than three minutes. Wikenhauser has attempted to explain this feature by granting the assumption that Luke gave "as a rule only short summaries of the main thoughts."[96] Yet if we study the speeches of Acts stylistically, we find that they certainly are not summaries or tables of contents. The features noted by Dibelius concerning Paul's famous Areopagus speech are more or less characteristic of all the speeches in Acts. They show "the style of a speech which was to be delivered. There is an intentional harmony between the beginning and the end; the apostrophe and the demonstration of proof are vivid; the formation of the sentences demands that they should be spoken aloud; many groups of words are adorned with rhetoric."[97] They simply cannot be blown up like a balloon to produce the original size and shape. The speeches already form perfect literary units in themselves.

4.) In order to hold the position that the speeches of Acts are true transcripts of speeches that were once actually delivered, one must likewise adequately explain the *difficulties deriving from the history of tradition.* C. F. Evans has rightly noted that a speech remains well known after 20 or 30 years only if in the meantime it were continually repeated and handed down. Such a process would be quite natural for the words of Jesus. But it is a big question whether the same applied for the speeches of the apostles.[98] Unlike the words of the Jesus tradition, the tranmission of individual apostolic speeches probably had no specific "Sitz im Leben" (life situation) in the Christian community. Obviously such was not the case with the ancient professions of faith or creeds (cf. 1 Cor 15:3ff.). But these creedal formulas certainly are not simple apostolic sermons delivered in a given concrete situation. And what is said here about apostolic speeches in general holds similarly for those of Paul. It would be hard to imagine that they were taken down in writing or immediately transmitted in oral form.[99]

5.) An attentive examination of the speeches in Acts shows that they are strongly marked by the theology of Luke himself. Consider the following example.

One of the most important elements of Luke's theological perspective is the emphasis on *the continuity between Jesus of Nazareth and the Church.* In fact it was his interest in this theme that stands out as one of the decisive reasons why he continued his gospel with a second book. No one before him had ever done such a thing! Now there are a good number of Lukan characteristics that serve this theme of continuity: the 40 day period beyond the time of Jesus' earthly life when he comes and goes among his apostles;[100] the close relationship between the Ascension and Pentecost established by Luke;[101] and above all the specially Lukan *idea of witness*[102] programmatically set forth in Acts 1. The true witnesses to Jesus are the twelve apostles, for they were chosen in the Holy Spirit by Jesus himself (Acts 1:2) and were present from the beginning at whatever Jesus did and taught (Acts 1:21,22). Thus by their preaching and ministry they guarantee continuity in the Church's development.

Now in nearly all of the missionary speeches of Acts, this

Lukan idea of the apostles as witnesses of Jesus stands out in rather stereotyped fashion, specifically in 2:32; 3:15; 5:32; 10:39,41; and 13:31. Hence wherever the witness formula emerges in the speeches, it is really Luke the theologian speaking and not Peter or Paul.

6.) The speeches of Acts contain frequent Old Testament citations. In these speeches, persons, who certainly spoke Aramaic, occasionally cite the Bible in a way that presupposes their knowledge of the Greek Septuagint version,[103] and not of the Hebrew text. Thus, for example, James offers a scriptural proof from the prophet Amos in his speech at the apostolic council; but the text he cites would be impossible to find in the Hebrew Bible.[104]

Haenchen rightly notes that it is quite obvious that James, in Jerusalem, did not cite a biblical proof text from the Greek Septuagint, especially since the Hebrew text excludes any reference to the point he wanted to prove. Thus Luke unabashedly puts his own understanding of the Greek version of the Bible into the mouth of a person of apostolic times.[105]

7.) In a number of instances, the speeches are interrupted by activities or reactions which are not those of the speaker. And this interruption always happens at the precise moment when what is essential to the speech has just been stated, and the speech has reached its culminating point. This procedure is most clear in the incident involving Paul in the temple court (Acts 22:1-21). A ruckus breaks out among the audience just as Paul cites the words of Christ: "Depart; for I will send you far away to the Gentiles." This statement is precisely the point the whole speech is intended to make, the veritable high-point of the speech, for it is supposed to show that the Gentile mission is willed by God. Similar examples are Acts 7:53f.; 10:43f.; 23:6f.; 26:23f.; and probably also 3:26f.; 5:32f.; 17:31f.; 19:27f. This technique of interruption once again shows to what extent the speeches of Acts are literary compositions.[106]

8.) Further, it is logical to assume that the speeches have to be read and understood from the viewpoint of those for whom they were originally intended. But for whom were they in fact originally intended? Only for those who supposedly heard them when they were delivered? Or are they meant chiefly for the readers of Acts? In other words, if Peter tells the community of the death of Judas (1:18), he would simply be telling his hearers something they knew about for some time. But the reader of Luke-Acts knows nothing as yet about it because Luke, unlike Matthew, does not mention in his gospel what happened to Judas.[107]

What this indicates is that quite frequently the speeches in Acts presuppose knowledge of a preceding *narrative text.* Without this knowledge the reader of the entire book cannot understand what is being said in a given speech. Those who would have heard these speeches for the first time would have found them incomprehensible. Thus the Jewish audience to whom Paul directs his speech in Acts 22 would have rightly wondered how Saul could have known about Ananias, or how Ananias could have known that Saul was the chosen of the God of the fathers. But because the reader already knows what is reported in Acts 9, he does not have these questions.[108] Luke has in fact divided up the Ananias episode. In chapter 22 he has to tell it from Paul's point of view; therefore he only mentions Ananias' words to Paul. But in chapter 9 he gives a detailed report of the dialogue between Ananias and Christ. Thus Paul's speech in Acts 22 evidently presupposes the narrative of chapter 9.[109]

9.) Dibelius has shown that the speeches fulfill an important function within the total composition of Acts. They underline a certain number of events as particularly significant for the historical development that unfolds, and they afford the reader with a "sense of direction" to follow the events that ensue.[110]

Thus the story of Cornelius[111] (which occurs before Paul begins preaching among the Gentiles) shows that God himself wills the evangelization of the Gentiles. Luke develops the fundamental meaning of the event in Peter's speech at Cornelius' house (10:34-43) and, above all, in Peter's speech in Jerusalem (11:5-17).

The Areopagus speech is also programmatic for Acts. Luke does not tell us anything about what Paul might have said at Philippi or Corinth. But he does report the speech to the Athenians. This is intended to indicate that the new faith has already reached to the center of classical Greece.

The moment when Paul completes his public missionary career marks a particularly important turning point in Acts. Paul leaves his mission field, and the period of his captivity soon begins. For Luke this is sufficient reason for a literary detour to tell of the merits of the great missionary once again. And he does this by means of the speech Paul delivers at Miletus (20:18-35). Paul's words of farewell show better than any other speech in Acts that the speeches are a *key and integral part of the composition of the whole book of Acts.*

10.) It is quite surprising that Luke reports only three of Paul's speeches,[112] during the course of his missionary career. Moreover, each of them is addressed to a different audience —Jews (13:16-41), Gentiles (17:22-31), and finally a Christian community (20:17-35). This precise selection is obviously not accidental. It points to a *second* function of the speeches in Acts, namely to show the reader *in terms of examples* how preaching took place in apostolic times. This is how Paul the "pastor" preached to Christian communities (at Miletus). And this is how Paul addressed himself to his fellow Jews at Antioch). And this is how Paul directed himself to Gentiles (at Athens).

This *typical* function of the speeches appears quite clearly in Peter's missionary sermons (2:14-40; 3:12-26; 4:8-12; 5: 29-32; 10:34-43). Dibelius,[113] Schweizer,[114] and Wilckens[115] have discovered that all of the aforementioned sermons (prescinding from slight inversions or abridgments) are constructed according to the same *basic pattern:*

I. An introduction which is linked to the concrete situation occasioning the speech
II. The proclamation of Jesus the Messiah
   a) the culpable action of the Jews with regard to Jesus
   b) the salvific action of God with regard to Jesus
III. Scriptural proofs
IV. An appeal to conversion and reception of salvation.

This item of information should not lead to the hasty conclusion that Peter always preached his missionary sermons according to this pattern. For the same structure also underlies Paul's speech in Acts 13:16-41. It is much more probable that the pattern derives from Luke, who uses it to tell his readers: "This is the Christian proclamation of salvation as it was preached from the beginning in the whole church.[116] This is the 'teaching of the apostles' (2:42)."

This tenth point on the characteristics of the speeches of Acts reveals how these speeches differ in fact from contemporary Hellenistic literary and historical compositions. For the speeches of Acts are much more than the rhetorical and stylistic exercises of a Hellenistic author. And in ultimate analysis, they are not intended solely to fulfill a purely literary function within the structure of the work taken as a whole. Rather they are themselves *sermons* and *addresses*[117] to the believing reader; they are intended to show him the ways of God and to announce the good news of salvation.

Thus when compared with the literary speeches of his contemporaries, Luke's speeches do in fact disclose something new and distinctive. On the other hand, the speeches of Acts certainly belong to the ancient category of literary speech, for as we have already seen, they could not have been delivered in the form that we now have them. Luke undoubtedly could have used various materials to compose them, like incidental bits of news, historical sources, and the like. At times he takes up a pre-existing composition and expands upon it.[118] And to a large extent he draws upon material handed down by the believing community.[119] But all this does not alter the fundamental fact that the speeches of Acts were composed by Luke himself.

Therefore—to return once again to the accounts of Paul's conversion—it is much more reasonable to ascribe the differences among the three accounts to the *creative literary activity and composition of the author,* Luke, and not to the addition of specific historical data (the conservative method) nor to different literary sources (the literary critical method). In any event, we still have to test whether or not the differing presentations of Paul's conversion can be explained more simply and with fewer hypotheses in this way.

But before proceeding to this task, I should like to note that there is another reason why I have delved so thoroughly into the speeches of Acts in this chapter. The reason is that these speeches quite emphatically indicate that one must first of all inquire into the *literary structure* or *form* of an ancient text before attempting to interpret that text. What did the ancient historian have in mind when he inserted a speech into his work? From what common form does the literary speech derive? How has this form been modified by the author in question? Without the constant consideration of such questions of literary form, the interpretation of any ancient text—not only speeches—must necessarily lead to erroneous conclusions. From all that has been said, the names used to designate this direction of biblical interpretation should now be understandable; it is called the *form-critical method* or the *form-historical method.*[120]

For the majority of biblical scholars, the form-critical approach is something obvious and self-evident. And as far as Roman Catholic biblical interpreters are concerned, Pius XII called upon them to use this method in his encyclical "Divino afflante spiritu."[121] The more recent instruction of the Pontifical Biblical Commission[122] once again and even more emphatically urged them to do so. Finally, the dogmatic constitution on divine revelation (*Dei Verbum*) of Vatican II sets forth the form critical approach as the normative Catholic approach to the Bible.[123]

We began the third part of this work with the study of a relatively large and extensive literary structure, the *speech*. But the Damascus accounts contain still other, but smaller, literary forms. We now turn to these. And they too reveal the creative compositional activity of Luke.

2. *The Apparition Dialogue*[124]

The three Damascus accounts in Acts differ notably from each other both in specific motifs as well as in general structure. And yet in their central sections, all the accounts contain a literary segment that is much the same—the dialogue between Christ and Paul (9:4–6; 22:7–10; 26:14–16). In the ensuing discussion, I shall call this section "the apparition dialogue." Is this part of the accounts a well defined piece of tradition which perhaps even goes back to eye witnesses?

If we arrange the apparition dialogue in sense lines, we can readily see a stable literary structure, especially in the text of Acts 9:4–6:

A1	. . . saying to him	introductory formula
A2	Saul, Saul!	address: double vocative
A3	Why do you persecute me?	question of Christ
B1	But he answered:	introductory formula
B2	Who are you, Lord?	question of Paul
C1	But he . . .	introductory formula
C2	I am Jesus, the one whom you persecute	self-presentation of Christ
C3	But rise and go . . .	Commission

There is a correspondance between A and C in the solemn character of the address (A2) and of Christ's self-presentation (C2) as well as in the verbal agreement of "Why do you persecute me?" (A3) and ". . . the one whom you persecute" (C2). Between these statements of Christ stands a human utterance, a response that is both question and answer. This triple division is very impressive. Christ addresses man; man responds; Christ speaks the last word. And in this last word he reveals who he is, and this self-revelation provides the basis or reason for the commission he sets forth. Man accepts the commission in silence.

This whole literary piece bears the marks of a composed and artistically stylized dialogue. If this be the case, we should look for literary parallels. Now an attentive reading of the Old Testament yields almost identically structured apparition dialogues. These are to be found in three passages: in the command given to Jacob by the "angel of the Lord" to return to his homeland (Gen 31:11-13); in God's exhortation to Jacob ordering him to go down into Egypt (Gen 46:2,3); and finally in the divine apparition to Moses in the burning bush (Ex 3:2-10). To see the common form in these texts better, consider the following tables comparing the Old Testament texts of Gen 46:2f. and 31:11-13 and the texts of Acts 9:4-6 and 26:14-16. The Old Testament texts are translated from the Septuagint because the text of Acts is more similar to that text of the Bible than it is to the Hebrew text.[125]

	Gen 46:2f.:	Acts 9:4-6:
A1 A2	. . . saying: Jacob, Jacob!	. . . saying to him: Saul, Saul!
B1 B2	But he said: What is (it)?	But he said: Who are you, Lord?
C1 C2 C3	Saying: I am the God of your fathers. Stop being afraid to go down . . .	But he: I am Jesus, the one whom you persecute. But rise and go . . .

	Gen 31:11-13:	Acts 26:14-16:
A1 A2	. . . he said to me: Jacob!	. . . saying to me: Saul, Saul!
B1 B2	But I said: What is (it)?	But I said: Who are you, Lord?
C1 C2 C3	And he answered: I am the God who appeared to you . . . But rise now . . .	And the Lord answered: I am Jesus, the one whom you persecute. But rise . . .

Obviously these passages have the same literary structure. The Old Testament apparition dialogues have the *double vocative* in the address,[126] the very brief *question asked by the man* involved, and then *the self-presentation of the one appearing,* followed by a *commission* imparted by the one appearing.

A shorter form of the apparition dialogue also occurs in the Old Testament; it lacks the self-presentation (C2). This modified form can be found in the narrative about the sacrifice of Isaac (Gen 22:1,2 and 22:11,12) and in the first revelation of God to the young Samuel (1 Sam 3:4-14). In the New Testament, this shorter form—just like the *long form*—occurs only in Acts, specifically in the vision of Ananias (Acts 9:10,11) and that of Cornelius (Acts 10:3-5). This obviously is quite remarkable. A comparison of this *short form* is also helpful:

	Gen 22:1-2:	Acts 9:10-11:
A1	. . . and he said to him:	. . . and he said to him:
A2	Abraham, Abraham!	Ananias!
B1	He anşwered:	He answered:
B2	Here I am!	Here I am, Lord!
C1	And he said:	And the Lord said to him:
C2	Take you son and go . . .	Rise, go . . .

As one can see, Gen 22:1,2 and Acts 9:10,11 agree almost verbatim. I have not presented the apparition dialogue in Acts 10:3-5 here, but it too is highly noteworthy. There Cornelius responds to the address of the angel with "What is (it)?" (*ti estin*). The Septuagint usually employs this formula in the *long form* of the apparition dialogue for man's response, hence for B2 (cf. Gen 31:1; 46:2; Ex 3:4). But in the apparition dialogue between Christ and Paul, instead of "What is (it)?" (*ti estin*), Acts has the more precise "Who are you?" (*tis ei*) (9:5; 22:8; 26:15). Still, in the Cornelius story the *ti estin* ("what is (it)?) emerges rather suddenly in 10:4, although we might have expected it previously in 9:5.

The conclusion we are forced to draw from these observations is rather clear. These passages in Acts have been patterned after the Old Testament form of apparition dialogue, specifically as presented in the Septuagint version. Obviously subsequent readers of the Old Testament who encountered the apparition dialogue form in the text were well aware that it was a fixed literary form used to tell of the appearance of God or of an angel. In fact the form could be re-applied to state the same message. Thus similar apparition dialogues occur in not a few passages of late Jewish literature. The *long form* is used in Jubilees 44:5; 2 Esdras 12:2-13; Apocalypse of Abraham 8:2-5; 9:1-5; Joseph and Aseneth 14:6-8. The *short form* can be found in Jubilees 18:1,2; 18:10,11; Apocalypse of Abraham 11:3-5; 12:6,7; 14:1-3; 14:9,10; 19:1-3; 20:1-3; Apocalypse of Moses 41; Testament of Job 3:1,2.

I will cite only one text from this listing, mainly because it is especially informative for our purposes. It is taken from the Jewish legend, *Joseph and Aseneth*.[127] The context of the passage is as follows. The archangel Michael appears to Aseneth, the future wife of Joseph, then in Egypt. The Archangel is sent to convert her because at the time she is still a pagan:

And behold, in the vicinity of the morning star, the sky opened and there appeared an indescribable light. And Aseneth fell upon her face to the ground. And to her came a men from heaven. He stood above her head and called to her: "Aseneth!" She answered "Who is it that calls me? For the door of my chamber is closed and the tower is high. How then has he entered my Chamber?"

A1 The man called to her again and said:
A2 *"Aseneth, Aseneth!"*
B1 And she answered:
B2 *"Here I am, Lord!* Tell me: *Who are you?"*
C1 And the man said:
C2 *"I am* the commander of the house of the Lord and commander-in-chief of the whole army of the Most High.
C3. *Get up on your feet,* and I will speak to you."

Note how easily and without contrivance the apparition dialogue has been applied to this text. This example clearly shows that the apparition dialogue form is essentially a literary device, a literary method of expression. For it is quite certain that the subject matter did not dictate that the apparition had to be described in this way. The Old Testament, in fact, contains many other passages telling how God appeared and spoke to various people,[128] but only five Old Testament texts are written in the style of the apparition dialogue form—the five previously cited. To verify how differently appearances can be described in the Bible, one need only read of the encounter of Yahweh with Abraham (Gen 18) in the Old Testament, or the meeting of the Risen Lord with the Emmaus disciples (Luke 24:13-31) in the New.

This prompts the question as to whether the apparition dialogue belonged to a previous tradition about Paul's conversion adopted by Luke,[129] or whether Luke himself introduced it into the Damascus story. In the first case, the description of the conversion of Paul would have already been shaped within the pre-Lukan tradition with the aid of an Old Testament literary form. In the second case, Luke himself would have drawn upon the Old Testament form to describe and interpret the encounter between Christ and Paul.

We have decided for the second possibility and this solely on methodological grounds. For if in the process of tradition a unique literary structure emerges (here: the apparition dialogue form), then this structure should not be localized at some vague "somewhere" in the tradition. Rather its origin should be located at the point where, to the best of our knowledge, editorial activity was most vigorous. In our case this point occurs specifically at the culmination of the tradition process, i.e., in the work of the author, Luke. The speeches of Acts are already proof enough of this.

Of course, it would be something else again if specific details in the apparition dialogues pointed to older levels of the tradition process. But such indications are not present in the texts. On the contrary, the notable fact that the apparition dialogue form occurs in Acts also *in passages other than* the accounts of Paul's conversion points to the hand of Luke. And this holds all the more so since the Damascus story (ch. 9) and the narrative about Cornelius' conversion (ch. 10, where the apparition dialogue also occurs) originally have nothing in common at all. It was Luke who quite purposely first put both traditions together to demonstrate how God initiated the mission to the Gentiles.[130] G. Stählin has well noted how both stories are structured in parallel fashion: ". . . both times the conversion occurs in two acts, the first of which is produced by means of a heavenly apparition (cf. 9:3ff. with 10:3ff.); and the second, by means of a divinely sent earthly emissary (cf. 9:10ff. with 10:24ff.). Moreover, at the beginning of the second act, in both instances there occurs a heavenly apparition (cf. 9:10ff. with 10:10ff.) by means of which the initial opposition of the

earthly messenger is overcome."[131] If to this we add the observation that within the whole New Testament, the apparition dialogue form occurs only in Acts, it would seem to
follow that these passages derive from the hand of Luke
and not from some anonymous community tradition. And
regardless of whether Luke himself or an older tradition be
at work here, in either case form critical-analysis demonstrates that the apparition dialogues are certainly not historical reports of what really happened between Christ and
Paul.

According to A. Girlanda *(Verbum Domini,* 1961) there are
various parts in the three conversion accounts that should be
distinguished from each other. The essential part would be
the apparition dialogue; it would contain *the historical event.*
The other parts of the various accounts—Girlanda refers especially to the variations and discrepancies—reveal the hand
of Luke and show how he subsequently interpreted the
event.[132] Girlanda's work represents an essay by a Catholic
that takes Luke's literary activity and theological creativity
quite seriously. And yet it must be said that the subject is
not as simple as Girlanda presents it. The reason for this is
that we really have no way to distinguish so neatly between
historical narrative and interpretation in these accounts. It is
precisely at those points where the three accounts almost entirely agree and where one might be led to think there is
something of the *historical* event present that the accounts
evidence a formally structured quality, hence that they are
interpretation.

Much like Girlanda, P. Gaechter has likewise drawn a
distinction between the historical account and the later interpretation.[133] He believes that our passages in Acts contain
Paul's subsequent reflection upon the apparition (26:16b-
18); the incidents appended to the apparition (Acts 9:10-
19; 22:12-16) stem from the tradition process. Yet all this

material must be sharply distinguished from the really historical nucleus of the accounts: "As far as the vision proper is concerned, all three accounts mutually agree. The narrative is entirely straightforward and without psychological and theological interpretation, and for this reason may be considered the original account of the apostle."[134]

This false appraisal of the apparition dialogue is instructive. It shows how careful one must be in attempting to infer the historicity of an account from its style and structure. Luke can in fact write in a simple and direct style, but this does not mean that what he writes is without his own theological interpretation or not shaped by his own purposes. The way in which he inserts the Old Testament apparition dialogue form into his material bespeaks not only literary ability (and this always demands reflection), but equally presupposes a requisite degree of theology.

3. The Mission Speech.

In both the first and second versions of the Damascus story, Christ's commission to Paul consists simply in sending him into the city: "But rise and enter the city, and you will be told what you are to do" (9:6); "Rise and go into Damascus, and there you will be told all that is appointed for you to do" (22:10).

But as we already know, in the third account this commission of Christ has become a formal mission speech in which Paul is sent directly to the Gentiles (Acts 26:16-18):

But rise and stand upon your feet; for I have appeared to you for this purpose, to appoint you to serve and bear witness to the things in which you have seen me and to those in which I will appear to you, delivering

you from the people and from the Gentiles—whom I
send you to open their eyes, that they may turn from
darkness to light and from the power of Satan to God,
that they may receive forgiveness of sins and a place
among those who are sanctified by faith in me.

At this point of our investigation, we shall present a separate form-critical consideration of Acts 26:16–18. To begin
with, note that the first part of the passage is a veritable
mosaic of citations from the prophets.[135] We find the following Old Testaments texts used here: a) *the vocation vision of
Ezechiel* (Ezechiel 1-2): "Stand upon your feet" is taken verbatim from Ezech 2:1. b) *the call of Jeremiah* (Jeremiah 1):
"I shall deliver you . . ." (26:17) derives from Jer 1:8: "I
am with you to deliver you says the Lord." The phrase in
Acts 26:17: ". . . from the Gentiles to whom I am now
sending you," is identical with a statement uttered by Christ
during Paul's vision in the Jerusalem temple, according to
Acts 22:21: "Depart, for I will send you far away to the
Gentiles." And both derive from Jer 1:7: ". . . for to all
to whom I send you you shall go." Further, Jer 1:5 certainly was a key reason for the choice of citing the call of
Jeremiah here.[136] The passage runs: "I appointed you a prophet *to the nations.*" (The Greek *"ethne"* is translated by
both "nations" and "Gentiles.") "To the nations" or "to
the Gentiles" (the same phrase in Greek: *eis ethne*) is perhaps the most pregnant phrase possible to characterize the
missionary work of Paul. Moreover, the catch phrase, "to
the Gentiles" *(eis ethne)* also marks the culminating point of
Paul's speech in the temple court.[137]

c) *the election of the Servant of God according to Isaiah 42:*
Compare Acts 26:18: ". . . to open their eyes that they
may turn from darkness to light," with Is 42:6-7: ". . . a
light to the nations, to open the eyes that are blind," and

Is 42:16: "I will turn the darkness before them into light."
Just like the phrase "to the nations" *(eis ethne)* in Jeremiah,
it seems most probable that "a light to the nations" (or Gentiles) *(eis phos ethnon)* is the key phrase pointing to and deriving from the Isaiah texts. Proof of this is furnished by the
express citation of Is 49:6 in Acts 13:47; there Paul says of
himself (and Christian missionaries in general): "For the Lord
has commanded us, saying: 'I have set you *to be a light for
the Gentiles,* that you may bring salvation to the uttermost
parts of the earth.'"

The aforecited reminiscences of Old Testament prophetic
texts, taken by themselves, certainly do not prove a direct
utilization of the Old Testament. But the facts that these
reminiscences are concentrated in the shortest space and especially that not *just one* of the great prophets, but three of
them are referred to, indicate to us that the Old Testament
is cited here in a conscious and purposeful way. Indeed, one
would have to say not only purposefully, but systematically
as well! For the reminiscence of Ezechiel derives from the
great *vocation vision* of Ezech 1-2; then passages from *the
call* of Jeremiah (Jer 1) are used twice. And while it is true
that Isaiah's vocation vision (Is 6) is not cited (it is cited two
chapters later in Acts 28:26,27), yet phrases from the *election*
of the Servant of God are. In other words, the mission
speech of Acts 26: 16-18 has been constructed of references
to the famous mission and vocation texts of the Old Testament—and this by Luke himself. This last point necessarily
follows once one accepts the fact that the apparition dialogue
form has been introduced by Luke. The reason for this is
that the mission speech of 26:16–18 is nothing else but an
expansion and extension of the commission C3.

Why did Luke arrange a series of citations from the Septuagint in his composition of the mission speech? We think
there are several reasons for this. The main reason behind the

selection of texts is the desire to write in a stylistically correct way; Jesus ought to speak *bibically*—and Luke's Bible was the Septuagint. Further, Jesus ought to speak in the language of the *Old Testament Lord (Kyrios)*; Jesus now speaks to Paul in the same way God once spoke to the prophets. This bespeaks not only compositional art, but theology as well. We shall later consider the theological ramifications of the fact that Paul is sent out by Christ like an Old Testament prophet.[138] At this point, we would simply like to note that anyone in the primitive Christian Church who might want to reflect on "vocation" would be almost forced by necessity to refer to the great Old Testament prophets. And certainly Jeremiah—who so penetratingly described how God himself sent him and urged him into his service—would not be overlooked.

Paul himself likewise interpreted the Damascus event with the help of Old Testament vocation texts. When in Gal 1: 15 he says of himself: "But when he who had set me apart before I was born and had called me through his grace, was pleased to reveal his Son to me. . . ," he has in back of his mind the call of Jeremiah (cf. Jer 1:15) and probably also the election of the Servant of God (cf. Is 49:11). However, the fact that Paul does indeed allude to these Old Testament texts does not necessarily mean, as some have concluded,[139] that the third account of Acts must stem from Paul. J. Munck believes that the early Christian community had a fixed tradition of applying vocation texts from Isaiah and Jeremiah to Paul,[140] but there are really no convincing reasons to bolster this view. Rather, the naturalness with which Paul considers his mission in the light of the great prophets indicates how readily this reference to the Old Testament suggested itself to early Christianity.

Inspite of all that has been said thus far, the form-critical investigation of the mission speech in 26:18 is still not finished. The reason for this is that the reminiscences of the Old Testament run only from verse 16 to the first part of verse 18. At that point the language of the passage changes in character. It no longer flows *directly* from the Old Testament, but now reveals features common to the *preaching language* of the early Christian church.[141] This can readily be seen especially from a comparison with Col 1: 12-14, which states: ". . . giving thanks to the Father, who has qualified us to share in the inheritance of the saints in the light. He has delivered us from the dominion of darkness and transferred us to the kingdom of his beloved Son, in whom we have redemption, the forgiveness of sins." Thus the following phrases appear both in Acts 26:18 and Col 1:12-14: "inheritance of the saints," "forgiveness of sins," and "the dominion of darkness." This does not mean that there is a literary dependence between the two passages, but rather that both have been influenced by the same early Christian way of speaking.[142]

4. The Double Vision.

According to Acts 9:10-16, Ananias has a vision in which he is ordered to seek out Paul. And Paul too has a vision in which he sees how a man named Ananias comes in to him and lays his hands on him so that he might see again. Now both of these visions are reported in an interesting way; they are not set down separately, one after the other, but one is being told *while the other is going on:* ". . . inquire in the house of Judas for a man of Tarsus named Saul; for behold, he is praying, and he has seen a man named Ananias come in and lay his hands on him so that he might regain his sight" (9: 11,12).

The way the two episodes are interwoven points once again

to the literary creativity of Luke. From verse 10 on, the scene is described from the viewpoint of Ananias. By using the literary device of having Christ himself describe what is meanwhile happening to Paul, Luke is able to avoid having to change the place of the action and the perspective of the narration. This literary procedure allows for an uninterrupted, dense, and flowing narrative. Luke uses the same literary technique in the Pentecost story. Naturally those participating in the event then did not say: ". . . And how is it that we hear each of us in his own native language? Parthians and Medes and Elamites and residents of Mesopotamia, Judea and Cappadocia, Pontus and Asia, Phrygia and Pamphylia, Egypt and the parts of Libya belonging to Cyrene and visitors from Rome, both Jews and proselytes, Cretans and Arabians, we hear them telling in our own tongue the mighty works of God! (Acts 2:8-11). Nobody talks this way. But the reason for this style of description lies in the author's intention to keep his narrative of the marvelous character of Pentecost intact, i.e., uninterrupted by a dry listing of nationalities. To inform his readers about all who were involved at the time, Luke simply puts the listing into the mouth of "the multitude."[143]

Thus, the interweaving of the two visions betrays the creative hand of Luke. To proceed further, we find that the double vision itself appears to be a distinct literary technique well attested in ancient literature. But since the double vision does not follow a specific, detailed pattern like the one found, for example, in the apparition dialogue, it is better not to refer to it as a literary form. Rather, we ought perhaps call it a literary motif.[144] A. Wikenhauser has collected a great number of examples of the double vision from ancient literary sources and published them in *Biblica* in 1948.[145] From his material[146] I choose an account which is found on one of the many papyri deriving from the ancient

Egyptian city of Oxyrhynchos.[147]

The author of the narrative is ill. It is night. He is suffering from high fever and pain in his right side. Lying in bed, he finally falls asleep after a bout with insomnia. Before this, he prayed to God to help him. His mother sits sleepless, watching at his side. The text now continues: "Suddenly she had a vision—and it was no dream or dozing reverie, for her eyes were wide open. But she did not see distinctly because the divine apparition filled her with terror, and this impeded her from looking too closely to contemplate the figure of the god[148] or one of his accompanying servants. He was someone of superhuman stature, clothed in brilliant linen, holding a book in his right hand. He regarded me, running his eyes over me from head to toe two or three times, and then he disappeared. My mother came to, and still trembling, she tried to waken me. Then she found that the fever had gone away and that I was covered with heavy perspiration. So with prayer, she honored the epiphany of the god; then she wiped me off and awakened me. And when she tried to tell me of the miracle of the god, I interrupted her and told her everything. *For what she had seen in reality, I beheld in a dream.* And since the pains which assailed me had now vanished because the god granted me a cure which effaced all pain, I praised his benefactions."

In this example, the motif of the double vision is stated quite clearly in the sentence: "For what she had seen in reality, I beheld in a dream." The recipients of the vision are situated in the same place, but one experiences the epiphany of the god in a dream, while the other experiences it as an apparition while wide awake. In other examples of such double visions, the recipients are spatially separated. But what is essential to the motif is that both of the visions or dreams *correspond with each other, refer to each other or, again, work together toward a single purpose or goal.*

In assessing this motif in Acts, we find it highly significant that the double vision is foreign to the literary methods of the Old Testament and Judaism; there are no instances of it either in the Old Testament or in Jewish literature. But it is typical of Hellenistic literature.[149] Consequently we have to presuppose that it was the "Hellenistic author," Luke, who was first to introduce the motif into the Damascus episode. This presupposition is further borne out by the fact that in the Cornelius story, one chapter later, a similar double vision is reported. Both Peter and Cornelius receive corresponding divine commands. Cornelius receives orders from an angel to have Peter fetched from Jaffa (10:1-6). While his messengers are approaching Jaffa, Peter is prepared for the meeting with Cornelius by a heavenly vision of a great tablecloth covered with various animals (10:9-16). In addition, the Holy Spirit simultaneously enjoins Peter to follow the messengers, now standing before the door, to Caesarea (10:19,20). Both visions along with the Spirit's injunction to Peter work together to the same end—the meeting of Cornelius and Peter, and the conversion of the first Gentile to Christianity.

The Cornelius story provides a good indication of what Luke seeks to attain with the motif of the double vision. He intends to show that at the time when the Church turned toward the Gentile mission, God himself was directing the course of events, step by step.[150] By means of his revelations to Cornelius and Peter, and to Paul and Ananias, God intervened directly into history and led the actions of men to his own ends. But when men experienced their visions from God, for the most part they did not have the faintest idea of what God intended by it all. They are told only: "And now send men to Joppa and bring one Simon who is called Peter!" (10:5). Or: "Behold, three men are looking for you. Rise and go down and accompany them without hesitation!" (10: 19,20). Or: ". . . he has seen a man named Ananias come in and lay his hands on him so that he might regain his sight" (9:12). Thus at that moment in time, Paul knew nothing of God's plan for him. God alone held all the strings in his hand, arranging everything with a view to the purpose he wished to accomplish—the mission to the Gentiles!

To say that Luke introduced the literary device of the double vision into the Damascus episode and the Cornelius story does not preclude the possibility that one or another vision narrative, taken singly, might be pre-Lukan.[151] The motif of a double vision is constituted by joining together transmitted visions or by composing a new vision to correspond with an existing traditional vision.

5. *A Greek Proverb.*

In comparison with the apparition dialogues of the first and second Damascus accounts, the third one in chapter 26 presents an interesting amplification. A new statement is added to the address: "Saul, Saul, why do you persecute me?", namely: "It is hard for you to kick against the goads?" (Acts 26:14). The sentence depicts an image well known to men of antiquity. It was senseless for a beast of burden to kick against the sharp goads of an animal driver, since that would only increase the pain. Now if we should apply this picture to Paul's life, it would be wrong to psychologize by imagining that it referred to Paul's kicking against invisible goads acting against his innermost conscience for such a long time with his fanatic persecutions.[152] What is meant, rather, is that what Paul had done against the Church, and therefore against Christ, was entirely senseless, and to resist against Christ now would be equally senseless. Christ is stronger than he is.

The reason for this explanation is that "to kick against

the goads" was a current Greek (and Latin) proverbial phrase used to signify useless resistance against a greater force or power. The phrase is attested to frequently since the time of Aeschylus.[153] But the phrase is totally lacking in Hebrew and Aramaic,[154] even though Semitic cultures also made use of goads to drive beasts of burden.

Since this is the case, must we admit that the exalted Christ used a Greek proverb? The question is more complicated than it might first appear. For what a person sees and hears in a vision is invariably perceived and understood in terms of the experiences provided by his own culture.[155] Hence, it is quite possible that this proverb about goads was used to give some concrete expression of the meaning of Paul's vision. The experience itself would have been quite inexpressible in human cultural terms.

However, in our case it seems more reasonable to admit that Luke put the well known, current Greek proverb into Christ's mouth to explain to his readers that no resistance on Paul's part was possible. There are two reasons in favor of this explanation: first, the form critical analysis of the context (the proverb stands within an apparition dialogue!); and second, the fact that Luke's report of Paul's speech in chapter 26 sparkles with many other high-class Greek expressions.[156] And we need not go far to find the reason for this high-class literary style here—in Acts 26 Paul addresses a royal audience, and not the Jewish masses as in Acts 22.

6. The Effect Produced by the Apparition.

At the conclusion of our form-critical investigation, let us take a look at the very different ways in which Luke describes the effect of the Damascus apparition on Paul and his companions. We have already seen that neither the literary critical solution nor the historicizing interpretation of conservative exegesis can really provide a satisfactory solution to this diversity.

Now in order to interpret the texts *objectively* here, it is once again necessary to recall that in antiquity, a whole range of stereotyped formulas and typical motifs were available for describing an apparition. Think of the legendary description of Michael's appearance to Aseneth[157] -the heavens open, a great light beams forth, Aseneth falls upon her face to the ground. All these features, along with many more, are attested to hundreds of times in Greek and Jewish literature.[158] Even the feature that only the person for whom the vision is intended actually perceives it is quite common.[159] A good example of this is provided by the account of the epiphany of the angel of revelation to Daniel (Dan 10:5-9):

> I lifted up my eyes and looked, and behold a man clothed in linen, whose loins were girded with gold of Uphaz. His body was like beryl, his face like the appearance of lightning, his eyes like flaming torches, his arms and legs like the gleam of burnished bronze, and the sound of his words like the noise of a multitude. And I, Daniel, alone saw the vision for the men who were with me did not see the vision, but a great trembling fell upon them, and they fled to hide themselves. So I was left alone and saw this great vision, and no strength was left in me; and when I heard the sound of his words, I fell on my face in a deep sleep with my face to the ground.[160]

This description, too, is outfitted with the typical motifs of light (lightning, torches), mighty voices, and finally, falling to the ground. Much like in the Damascus episode, here too the seer's companions are aware that something unheard of and marvelous is taking place, yet they do not participate in the actual apparition.[161]

When set before this background of stereotyped formulas and typical motifs, the differences within the varied accounts of the Damascus story lose importance. One account reports: "they heard the voice, but saw no one"; the other: "they saw the light, but did not hear the voice." While these opposing features ought not be simply dismissed without explanation, yet neither ought they be ranked as formal contradiction. The *center of meaning* of both statements consists in this, that although Paul's companions do perceive that an apparition is taking place, they cannot participate in it the way Paul does. Luke makes this point by using different turns of expression. The turns of expression change, but not the meaning of the statement.[162]

The same observation holds for the merely apparent contradiction concerning the posture of Paul's companions. At one time Paul's fellow travelers stand around him petrified with terror, while at the other, they are prostrated on the ground with Paul. In both instances, different literary devices current in the ancient world are used to express the same idea, namely, the might and fascination which seizes even Paul's companions at the appearance of Christ.[163] Once again, it should hardly take further proof to conclude that it was Luke himself who variously depicted the effect of the apparition on Paul and his companions in this way, yet always with a view to pointing up the same central meaning of the episode.

7. *Literary Forms and Historical Truth.*

We have come to the end of our form-critical observations

on the Damascus story, yet they are by no means complete. For there are many other form-critical questions that might be considered. For example, is the Ananias episode (9:10-19; 22:12-16) based upon an originally independent narrative whose central point was healing of the blind Paul? This is what Trocmé contends.[164] In his view, the description of what happened on the road to Damascus really only serves as a brief introduction to the event proper, the healing; and this healing is described according to the then current pattern of the Synoptic healing accounts.

Be that as it may, I shall not pursue the question any further here. For by and large what concerns us now is quite clear—the three descriptions in Acts of Paul's conversion are not historical, verbatim transcripts containing detailed data of what exactly happened. Moreover, these accounts do not derive from a simple editorial process whereby Luke would have just worked different historical sources together. Any interpretation of the Acts passages based upon such a presupposition will necessarily be wrong. The reason for this is that in the final analysis, we are dealing with creative literary compositions, constructed of different patterns and forms. And Luke himself was chiefly responsible for the resulting composition.

Many people who hear something like this for the first time quickly jump to false conclusions and mistaken judgements. These are well known: "If that is true, then everything in Acts is unhistorical!" "Is anything really true in the Bible?" "Did anything really happen at all to Paul?"

The fact is that when the form-critical method is correctly understood, it most certainly does not lead to the conclusion that everything in our biblical texts is unhistorical. What have we really established by form-critical analysis? The effect of the Damascus apparition is described in terms generally used in the 1st century A.D. Luke put a Greek proverb into Christ's mouth to describe Paul's situation, and this proverb was well known and understood at the time. Christ's mission speech to Paul is fashioned after the mission texts of Old Testament prophetic books. The apparition dialogue follows a literary form to be found already in the Old Testament. All these features point to the author's employment of well known literary forms, hence to his literary technique. Now to isolate and identify certain literary forms does not entail a judgement on the *historicity* or *non-historicity* of the events described. For it is entirely possible for quite accurate historical materials to be set down in different specific literary forms.[165] Just as a given writer's *individual, characteristic style* need not mutilate the truth he intends to describe, so also the *common literary style* of a given historical period or a specific circle of writers need not produce a distortion of historical facts. What we have in fixed literary forms is the common literary style of a given historical period.

Evidently, the fact that a specific literary compositional technique is being used frequently enables us to conclude that the event described certainly did not take place *in that outward form*. For example, Christ certainly did not utter that Greek proverb we have been talking about. Yet to note this does not settle *the question of the historical truth* of the incident. This question really entails much more than the observable course of events. Allow us to illustrate what we mean with an example.

Say there was a big traffic accident on the main street of a certain city. This accident can be described in various ways. A policeman might simply fill out his cut-and-dry forms. A student of traffic problems might include select facts of the accident in a study he is preparing. A writer, who happened to be an eye witness, might develop what he saw into a short story. The three descriptions of the accident would differ considerably. The literary forms used in each description would be entirely different. And yet in all three cases, the historical reality of the accident can be reported without distortion.

The police forms would probably contain just the bare and sober facts—time of day, direction of the vehicles, length of tire marks, type of car, license number, and the like. The writer might say nothing about all these items. The elements of his story might rather derive from something he could never have known simply by observing this particular accident. And yet it is possible that precisely because of these additional elements, the writer may more insightfully describe the ramifications of the accident (e.g., the homicidal nature of today's traffic) and thereby depict the accident much better. In this way, he perhaps grasps the significance of the concrete accident at a level that simple cannot be put into a police report or that no unreflecting eye witness to the accident might expect.

Evidently many of us today have been conditioned to think that the best forms for describing and understanding history are mainly statistics, official reports or "objective" surveys and polls. This attitude derives from the heavy influence which science and its quantity orientation and operational definitions has had on historical method. Now if history is just a sequence of measurable details and empirical facts, then one would have to concede that the best possibilites for understanding history are provided by vital statistics, census reports, calenders of events and sterile chronicles or log books. But even this posture entails noticeable difficulties. For the chronicler and pollster, too, have to choose their data from the chaotic succession of facts churned out during every day and every year of so-called history. Now what principles actually govern this selection? And if the facts thus sifted out are classified according to a certain "course of events," does not the process itself already presuppose a high degree of interpretation?

History is more than a classified collection of empirical

happenings and facts.[166] It always develops from and through the free actions of men, actions which ever remain in some way opaque to ultimate analysis. Because of this, history takes on a dimension of depth which just cannot be grasped without *interpretation and explanation.* How much could I get to know about a person if I were limited only to his photograph, the data on his I.D. and his *curriculum vitae?* Very little! And I would get to know just as little about history if I were limited to a knowledge of the empirical and observable course of events. (As I previously mentioned, the norms for determining and defining what data would comprise the so-called facts of this observable course of events are quite subjective. For example, have wars actually been as important as the space allotted to them in history books might lead us to believe?) The knowledge and understanding of history—just like the knowledge and understanding of a fellow human being—requires and presupposes empathy, interpretation and involvement. And for a historian to express these qualities of empathy and interpretation, he still must employ literary means of expression in his work that would be different from an accident report or a statistical survey.

Now what if an author intended to write about not just human history, but about *salvation history,* that is to describe how God leads history along to man's salvation, how God works in the depths of the human heart and reveals his salvation, and how man responds to these divine overtures by consenting to them or rejecting them. What would be the outcome of his work if he only reported the observable course of events he considers significant? Let us give our imagination free rein for the moment and say that the Damascus event were filmed in a perfectly objective way. Then say we were to see the film. What would we learn about the event from seeing the film? Certainly lots of details not to be found in either Acts or Galatians. But would we learn anything of the significance of the event proper? Certainly not from a documentary film! For the significance of an event does not emerge on the surface of the observable course of events, and what might perhaps appear to be extraordinary to us would still remain ambiguous. In other words, sheer documentary evidence would still leave us hanging; observable phenomena would remain mute; and *the event would still have to be explained and interpreted.*

Now what Luke intends to do it so explain and interpret. This task is the focus of his interests. To be sure, he did not append a second book to his gospel just to provide his readers with an empirical "Outline of the History of Primitive Christianity," or to compile the biographies of the apostles for prosperity. Rather he intends to lead his readers beyond empirical events and to give them an in-depth view of history, in which God himself is at work. Individual happenings thus became transparent and allow the non-empirical "directional meaning"[167] of the events to come through.

Consequently, a reader of Luke has to understand the author's real purpose before he can possibly question the historical truth of the work. Likewise, the reader has to assess the literary forms and devices used by Luke from the perspective of his purpose. It is not enough to state that these literary forms and techniques were understood and considered quite legitimate in his day and age. For we must also add that these forms and techniques were certainly not the worst available to describe the reality in question.

Perhaps this whole discussion will become clearer if after this more general and basic section, we go on to consider in greater detail the goals Luke set for himself.

8. The Goals That Luke Set for Himself.

Let us begin with a preliminary question. What concrete materials from tradition did Luke have to work with to help him realize his project?

One thing is certain; Luke knew from tradition that Christ appeared to that persecutor of Christians, Paul. But we can no longer reconstruct in any detail how this tradition went. It certainly contained names: Damascus, Ananias, and Judas. But did Luke have separate reports containing these names, or did he find them in an organized account of the event? Did Luke compose the Damascus story from the common knowledge of his time plus a series of additional separate reports, or did he already possess a larger, more extensive written or oral account which he could then edit? Since it has been shown that the very kernel of the Damascus story in Acts derives from Luke (the apparition dialogue form), a clear answer to such questions becomes more difficult.

Yet I believe it to be highly improbable for Luke to have composed such a large and varied narrative as the Damascus story without some coherent, organized prototype. Now there are some reasons that favor such a prototype. Gal 1:22,23 presupposes the existence of stories about the one-time persecutor among the communities of Judea.[168] Did this information circulate only in the form of brief reports? Or must we assume the existence of more extensive narratives, not only for Judea but for other regions as well? Then, there is the question of the source of information for Paul's being blinded and healed. These items are certainly pre-Lukan because in his third account, Luke demonstrates that he is capable of describing Paul's vocation without the blinding and subsequent healing. Then, too, the healing incident is closely connected with the name of Ananias. If all these observations are correct, then we not only have reached back to a pre-Lukan stage of tradition, but must likewise presuppose the existence of a coherent narrative since the description of the blinding and healing already form a fixed narrative strand.

Perhaps we can move even further. If a blinding is described in the context of an apparition of Christ, it could hardly have been caused except by a light from heaven. If this be true, then did mention of the light also belong to Luke's prototype? And would not the light require a corresponding heavenly voice? But what did this voice say?. . .We thus gradually move into a field of uncontrollable conjectures. But this brief excursion into the history of the tradition process does confirm what we have said at the very outset—we can no longer produce a detailed reconstruction of the shape of the tradition which Luke reworked. Probably a real narrative lies at the bottom of it, but that is really not certain.

Be that as it may, Luke did know from tradition (in what form matters little) that Paul had a vision of Christ near Damascus and that the vision moved the one-time persecutor to redirect his life. He also used the available traditional information about Paul's conversion. But he also interpreted this information and explained it in terms of its significance for the history of the Church. What points of view, then, gave direction to his work, and how have they influenced the shape of his composition?

To begin with, the Damascus story has *extraordinarily great* significance for Luke's work. He tells it no less than three times, surely not to fill up space as J. Wellhausen thought,[169] but to impress it upon his readers, as though saying: "Here you have one of the especially important events of my book!"[170] But how, more specifically, does Luke view the significance of this event? The Cornelius story provides an indication, because like the Damascus story, it too is repeated two more times. It is first reported in chapter 10; almost immediately afterwards Peter tells it again at length (11:5-15): finally Peter alludes to it at the apostolic council (15:7-9). What leads Luke to emphasize these events by means of *the literary technique of repetition* is, in both instances, the significance of the events for the Gentile mission. With the Damascus apparition, God calls the future great missionary to the Gentiles as a "chosen instrument" (9:15). With the conversion of Cornelius by means of Peter, God himself inaugurates the mission to the Gentiles.

Thus the repetition of the Damascus story does call the reader's attention to the importance of the event for subsequent history. But this is not its sole function. For repetition allows an author like Luke the room necessary for a discussion of some principal questions which are closely connected to his theme. Repetition enables him to consider issues bound up with the mission to the Gentiles, and to fit this discussion into the Damascus story. For example, from where did the Christian Church get the right to carry on missions among the Gentiles? Was not the abandoning of circumcision an apostasy from the Jewish faith? What about the continuity of God's plan of salvation if such a profound schism emerged between Judaism and the early Church?[171]

Luke responds to these questions chiefly, but not exclusively, in the second and third accounts. By strongly emphasizing Paul's strict Jewish orthodoxy[172] and his zeal as persecutor of Christians,[173] Luke makes it abundantly clear that Paul would never have undertaken his mission to the Gentiles on his own. It was the irresistible power of Christ alone that led him to it. The transfer of God's Gospel from the Jews to the Gentiles did not derive from human calculation or design, but was in God's plan from the beginning. In fact God himself set the process underway. Thus the Church among the Gentiles—already a notable phenomenon in Luke's day—was not an apostasy from the Old Testament, but rather the fulfillment of the Old Testament if considered from the vantage point of salvation history. Consequently, the heated attacks of Judaism against the Church are unfounded.

We now wish to go a bit deeper into Luke's intentions, and this insofar as they are expressed in the literary forms used in the Damascus story.

Luke intends to describe the irresistible might of Christ that proceeds from his appearance to Paul and that ultimately drives Paul to the Gentile mission. He achieves this goal by using various means. First of all, there is the light which envelops Paul. It does not matter whether this feature of the narrative is pre-Lukan or not; Luke has consciously and intentionally exaggerated it.[174] The power of this light is revealed in the blinding of the persecutor: ". . . and when I could not see because of the brightness of that light" (22:11). —In the third account, Luke replaces the blinding of Paul and Ananias' cure with the fall of Paul's traveling companions.[175] This fall also expresses Christ's might.—And the Greek proverb in 26:14 belongs here as well. It shows that there is no resisting Christ. —The apparition dialogue serves the same end, but in a somewhat different way. The literary form, fixed in the Septuagint version, allows for only a short question from the recipient of the apparition. But the development of the dialogue is dominated by the mighty self-presentation of the one appearing, and especially by the command which closes the dialogue and which brooks no resistance.[176] —Finally, Paul's words to Agrippa have to be understood in the light of all these descriptive techniques: *"Wherefore,* O King Agrippa, I was not disobedient to the heavenly vision . . ." (26:19). In other words, Paul could not do otherwise; he was driven to the Gentile mission by the irresistible might of the Messiah.

Furthermore, Luke intends to demonstrate that not only does the Gentile mission derive from the divine will —and not the will of men—but God himself moved the Gentile mission along by intervening at each of its crucial stages. To this end, he arranges a whole series of direct divine interventions in chapter 9 and 10, and they are described in such a way that the course of events really unfolds only due to these continuous interventions:

9:3-7:	Christophany to Paul:
	Order to enter the city.
9:10-16:	Ananias' vision:
	Order to go to Paul.
9:12:	Paul's vision:
	Paul sees Ananias coming.
10:1-6:	Cornelius' vision:
	Order to fetch Peter.
10:10-16:	Peter's vision:
	Insight that the Gentiles are not unclean.
10:19,20:	Exhortation through the Spirit to Peter:
	Order to follow Cornelius' messengers.
10:28:	Allusion to Peter's vision (10:10-16).
10:30-32:	Report of Cornelius' vision (10:1-6).
10:44-46:	The Holy Spirit comes upon Gentiles,
	manifesting his presence by outward signs.

The literary motif of the double vision[177] plays an important part within these continuous divine interventions. To a great extent it makes visible how God moves events along step by step and directs them according to his own plan.

Moreover, Luke also intends to show that the promises of the Old Testament are fulfilled with the Gentile mission. Thus in the mission speech of the third account (26:16-18), Luke has Jesus pronouncing the words with which the Lord *(Kyrios)* of the Old Testament sent forth his prophets, words which even in those days spelled out the universalism of salvation. From the string of citations from the prophets in 26:16-18, some scholars have concluded that Luke thereby intended to depict Paul *as a prophet.*[178] However, the texts do not bear out this conclusion. Consider the fact that in 26:17,18 and the allusions to Jeremiah and Isaiah, the key role is played by the phrases "to the Gentiles" *(eis ethne)* and "a light to the Gentiles" *(eis phos ethnon).*[179] The main emphasis here is not on prophet, but on Gentiles. With these allusions, Luke wants to intimate that by the fact of Paul's bringing the Gospel to the pagans, the Old Testament prophetic promises are fulfilled. That Luke makes this statement in the context of a mission mandate—on the occasion marking the beginning of Paul's missionary activity—ought not throw us off the track. The fact is that with chapter 26 Luke already draws near the end of his book. The public missionary work of Paul has long since come to an end in the literary plan of Acts (cf. 20:17-38). And if the mission mandate is retold at this point, the reason for it here is to offer the reader a summarizing and insightful backward glance on what already took place in Paul's work among the Gentiles—namely the Old Testament has been fulfilled.[180]

All the foregoing considerations still leave us far from adequately grasping the literary and theological ends that Luke set for himself, insofar as they are expressed in the concrete accounts of the Damascus story. But even this sort of inquiry has its limits. For the better an author composes his work and on the more levels he proceeds, the less is it possible to analyse and reduce his composition into "themes" and "ideas." But that certainly has not been our purpose. This section is meant chiefly to show how Luke attempted to present a deeper understanding of a single event and to view it in a salvation-history context. It also aims to highlight the extent to which Luke's literary procedures are already interpretation and explanation.

9. Luke's Talent as Writer.

Luke, therefore, interprets events. If this is what he set out to do, he could have presented his interpretation in sterile and abstract words, scattered through the text as "reflections" of the author. But that would have made for tedious reading, and Acts would have lost all forcefulness and vividness.

Luke goes about it differently. He tells a story; he narrates a history. And he does so with a talent for composition unheard of in the early Church. His fine literary insights dictate that he should not tell the same story three times with the same words;[181] not even his ancient audience would allow for this, since they measured an author's abilities by his skill at variation. And Luke is such a skilled author. If we but compare the three Damascus accounts, we can readily see how Luke varies his vocabulary with a view to enlivening the presentation. In 9:6 Christ says to Paul: "Go *into the city*," but in 22:10: "Go *into Damascus*." —Paul receives letters to the synagogues of Damascus once *from the highpriest* (9:1f), then *from the council of elders and the highpriest* (22:5), and finally *from the highpriests* (26:12; 9:14).—Luke has an abundance of names for Christians. Paul persecuted *the disciples of the Lord* (9:1), *those who were of the Way* (9:2), or simply *the Way* (22:4) or *the saints* (26:10). Besides these, chapter 9 also mentions *the brethren* (9:17,30) and *those who call upon the name of Christ* (9:14,21). —The designation of Paul's companions is likewise carefully varied: 9:7 calls them *fellow travelers (synodeuontes)*; 22:9: *those who were with him*; and 26:13: *those who journeyed with him (poreuomenoi)*. This should be sufficient sampling to illustrate how well Luke varies his vocabulary and phraseology within the three accounts.[182]

There is still another type of variation which Luke uses: he artfully intensifies the accounts as he moves from one to another. For example, consider the description of the light: chapter 9 simply states: *a light* from heaven flashed about him (v. 3); in chapter 22 Luke intensifies it: *a great light* flashed about him (v. 6); but the high-point is reached in chapter 26: *a light brighter than the sun* appears, shining from heaven (v.

13). But that is not all; in the first account he does not tell
his readers when the apparition took place, but in the second
and third accounts we find that it took place "about noon"
(22:6) and "at midday" (26:13). Does this information about
the time of day really have "the casualness of personal recollection" as Hirsch maintained; and must this trait therefore
derive from "oral tradition stemming from Paul"?[183] A purely
literary explanation seems much more obvious. By making
reference to the time of day, Luke just wants to intensify the
brilliance of the light; it was not bright because it stood before a dark background, but on the contrary, it was so bright
that it made the noon day sun pale by comparison.[184] This
explanation is further bolstered by the fact that the light
motif undergoes still further intensification. According to 9:3
and 22:6, the light flashed only around Paul, but according
to 26:13, it also affects his companions.

Now while Luke makes the brilliance of the apparition grow
brighter from account to account, he does just the opposite
in his description of Paul's activity as persecutor. He paints
this activity with increasingly darker colors. The texts just
about speak for themselves:

1. "But Saul laid waste the church, and entering house
after house, he dragged off men and women and committed them to prison" (8:3).[185]

2. "I persecuted this 'Way' to the death, binding and delivering both men and women" (22:4).

3. "I not only shut up many of the saints in prison, by
authority from the chief priests, but when they were put
to death, I cast my vote against them. And I punished
them often in all the synagogues and tried to make them
blaspheme; and in raging fury against them, I persecuted
them even to foreign cities" (26:10,11).

The intensification in the third account is unmistakable. The reader here learns for the first time that Paul himself imprisoned Christians,[186] while previously we are told only that he "delivered" them. Finally, the third account tells us that he tried to make Christians blaspheme and persecuted them even to foreign cities. And the item about Paul taking part in the killing of Christians (other than Stephen in 8:3) is entirely new, but prepared for in 22:4 ("and persecuted to the death").[187]

This carefully thought out technique of intensification is also found at work in the mission charge to Paul. According to chapter 9, Paul is selected "to carry my (Christ's) name before the Gentiles and kings and the sons of Israel" (v. 15). This sentence is almost always interpreted wrongly.[188] It does not mean that Paul is *to bring the name of Christ to Gentiles and Jews,* but that he is *to confess the name publicly before Gentiles and Jews.*[189] The phrase refers to the concrete situation of persecution and public arraignment.[190] Consequently Paul's missionary activity proper (missionary journeys, founding new Christian communities, etc.) stands far in the background at 9:15. Besides, Christ's explanation of Paul's fate here is intended primarily for Ananias, for it is meant to answer his difficulties in accepting Paul. The person who still goes around persecuting those who profess the name of Christ (9:14), dragging them off to court, will himself be arraigned in various courts and there profess the name of Christ. Whether Ananias informed Paul of Christ's words or not is left open by Luke. In sum, then, the first Damascus account states that Paul is called to be a Christian, and this is clearly expressed; but nothing is said yet about a mission.

This perspective changes in the second account. There Ananias tells Paul: "The God of our fathers appointed you . . . for you will be a witness for him to all men of what you have seen and heard" (22:14,15). This statement is much closer to a mission charge, since the terminology is just like that in Acts 1:8 ("you shall be my witnessess"). And yet there is no sending on a mission in the strict sense. —The temple vision in 22:17-21 marks a further intensification. Christ himself, not Ananias, now speaks to Paul. Now for the first time, there is mention of Paul's being sent on a mission: "Depart, for I will send you far away to the Gentiles!" (22:21). But even this statement of Christ's is still not the mission charge itself. According to the wording of the text, the mission change still lies in the future.

Chapter 26 brings us to the climax of the development. Now finally Paul is actually sent forth, and this immediately by Christ and directly outside Damascus.

By employing this literary technique, Luke has Paul's mission charge become the object of sharper and more direct focus with each account. But there is also a gradual tightening and concentration of the narrative which accompanies this intensification of content.[191] The Damascus story proper in chapter 9 consists of 17 verses (9:3-19); that in chapter 22, of only 11 verses (22:6-16), while that in chapter 26 has only 7 verses (26:12-18). All these features clearly point up to Luke's literary sensibility, always keeping the three accounts together in a perceptible inner relationship. His narrative talent could be further illustrated with many other examples. But what has been said should suffice. For we still have to discuss a problem mentioned at the beginning of this study. This problem deals with the several, considerable differences between Acts and the Pauline letters relative to the Damascus apparition.

10. Acts and the Statements in the Letters of Paul.

Let us recall that Paul claimed to be an apostle; but for Luke, the office of apostle is limited to the Twelve. Paul ranks his call among the Easter appearances of Jesus; Luke clearly distinguishes it from them. Paul emphasizes that he received his call immediately from God. In Luke's perspective, at least according to the first two accounts, there was mediation on the part of Paul's fellow Christians.

If exegetes were just historians, they could simply dismiss these differences as contradictions, like those often encountered among various source documents. But they are not just historians, but also theologians. And therefore they consider the Bible not merely as a collection of various writings from the past. For them the Bible is always Sacred Scripture, i.e., both a collection of books and *a unique and single book* in which God speaks his word. Thus biblical interpreters feel obligated to dig deeper into the texts to uncover the inner unity behind what at first glance might seem to be disparate elements.

But this in no way means their task is to explain away or harmonize all discrepancies in the Bible as quickly or as easily as possible. On the contrary, their first duty is to take all these differences quite seriously, and to investigate the theological positions taken by each individual book. By following such a procedure, it can often be proved that two statements which at first seem contradictory really belong to different "frames of reference," and therefore ought not be assessed by the same norms.

What I mean by the "frame of reference" can be best explained here in terms of our specific question. If Paul is of the conviction that he is an apostle of Jesus Christ, it is because he bases himself primarily upon an apparition of the resurrected Lord, in which God revealed his Son to him for the purpose of evangelizing the Gentiles. Paul sees the real origin of his apostolate in this experience (cf. 1 Cor 9:1). Now if we were to analyze all the passages, in their contexts, where Paul stresses his office of apostle, we would quickly see that what concerns him is *the legitimacy of his preaching.*[192] —What does Luke have to say? He, too, stresses that the apostles saw the risen Lord and that they received a mission charge from him.[193] But that does not suffice to qualify a person as an apostle. The Lukan apostle must have accompanied Jesus during his entire public ministry, beginning with the baptism of John (Acts 1:21,22; 13:31). Only in this way could the apostles be "witnesses to all the things he did both in the country of the Jews and in Jerusalem" (Acts 10:35). Luke's view, therefore, sharply differs from Paul's, since Paul was not a witness to the public ministry of Jesus. And yet all that this really proves is that in his conception of "apostle," Luke is really concerned about the continuity between the time period of Jesus and the time period of the Church. Now this theme of continuity is totally absent in the writing of Paul, at least in this form, because Paul is just not interested in the life of the earthly Jesus in the Lukan sense (cf. 2 Cor 5:16).

What we have just explained should certainly clarify what we mean by differences in frames of reference. To understand an individual concept, it is insufficient to treat it in isolation; rather one must consider its context and setting within the specific purposes intended by a given author. The Lukan idea of apostle always refers back to the time of Jesus—and so it bears different features than Paul's idea. Given a different frame of reference, identical words can be used to express entirely different conceptual backgrounds. The denotations might be similar, but the connotations are quite distinct.

We have to realize that during the period of its inception, the early Christian movement did not possess a collection of fixed, constant, and precise theological terms to which it could refer and from which it could be supplied with the proper labels for everything. As a matter of fact, such is not even the case today—and it would not be worth the effort to produce such a collection. In most cases, the primitive Church had to search for and reapply the terms with which it interpreted the mystery of Christ or the meaning of the Church. In part, the New Testament mirrors this attempt at the development of early Church terminology.

There is also a *second difference* that should cause us to pause before evaluating discrepancies between Paul and Luke with the same yardstick. This second point is that Paul ranks his call among the Easter appearances of Christ, while Luke removes it from that context.

The fact that Luke does not count the Damascus apparition among the Easter appearances of Jesus is logically in keeping with his description of the post-Easter period in Acts 1. According to this description, Jesus appears among his apostles over a 40 day period, proves to them that he really has been raised, and speaks to them of matters concerning the kingdom of God (Acts 1:3). The Ascension then follows, and with it Jesus definitively removes himself from among his disciples. But at the same time, the Ascension makes the coming of the Spirit at Pentecost possible.[194] The period of the Church now begins. By using the 40 days as a sacred interim period during which Jesus still moves about among his disciples, a period immediately followed by the Ascension and Pentecost, Luke is able to portray the continuity between the period of Jesus and the period of the Church in a highly graphic way. But we have to realize to what extent this description really serves Luke's theological interests, and simultaneously interprets and schematizes what actually happened after Easter.[195]

Paul's story of the appearances of Jesus in 1 Cor 15: 5-8 reveals no traces of contact with the Lukan outline of events (or the Matthaean [cf. Mt 28:16-20] or Johannine [cf. Jn 20:19-23] ones either for that matter). What this means is that Luke's understanding of the Damascus appearance must be explained in terms of his frame of reference, i.e., in view of his outline of the post-Easter period.[196] In Luke's frame of reference, the Damascus Christophany simply is not an Easter appearance.

The *third difference* that we have pointed out between Luke and Paul looks to the question of the immediacy of Paul's call. Paul insists that he did not receive his call and gospel from men, but from Jesus Christ.

The closest Luke comes to describing such a direct and immediate call from Jesus is in Acts 26. But as we have seen, what Luke does here is intensifies the theological utterance while at the same time abridging the narration of the event. Hence what Luke wants to say in chapter 26 is that Paul's missionary work was *willed by God himself*—and this certainly is not the immediate and direct call Paul has in mind in Galatians.[197] Luke just did not know what Paul wrote in that letter. We need not consider the function ascribed by Luke to Ananias in the first two accounts, that is, whether Luke considered him a formal representative of the Chruch or not. For as far as Luke knew, Paul always was in contact and communication with the Church, especially during the first phases of his work. Shortly after the event at Damascus, Barnabas presents him to the apostles in Jerusalem (9:27), and Paul lives among them (9:28). This obviously contradicts the statements of the epistle to the Galatians.

However, the contradiction loses much of its sharpness if we consider why Luke, for example, so stresses the interdependence between Paul and the apostles in Jerusalem. Certainly not to put down Paul, but rather to establish the legitimacy of his later missionary work.[198] And this is precisely what Paul ultimately intends to prove in Galatians. But he does so with arguments that are just the opposite!

Hence Luke does not report the concrete situation correctly —after all, he had no better information about it—and yet he is not all that far from Paul in what he intends to show.

In sum, although Luke's retrospective view derives from his own historical and theological perspective, which is different from Paul's, in many respects Luke and Paul are surprisingly close. Although Luke does not rank the Damascus vision among the Easter appearances of Jesus, his description of the event incomparably surpasses anything else that he relates in Acts about visions and revelations. And while Paul is not an apostle according to Luke, yet the greatness of his call and the exemplary character of his missionary activity are so masterfully depicted by Luke that in the end Paul stands almost equal to the apostles. Indeed, it is to Paul that the Isaiah text refers: "I have set you to be a light for the Gentiles, that you may bring salvation to the uttermost parts of the earth" (13:47). Luke could not use this mode of speaking and say anything similar of any of the apostles.

Conclusion

In conclusion, I would like to offer a brief statement on the relationship between the Lukan Damascus story and historical reality:

The report in Acts is not an exact verbal transcript of what really happened, yet it certainly is not pure fiction either. Rather it is both a report of a well attested historical tradition (cf. the Pauline letters) as well as Luke's interpretation and explanation of this historical tradition presented in conventionally accepted literary forms and literary techniques.

Having said this much, I still have something else to add. For some people, the Bible is simply a collection of ancient books. But for those for whom it is the "Sacred Scripture" in which the faith and self-understanding of the Christian movement have been set down, Luke's interpretation of events is not just his personal opinion, it is not just one of many possible interpretations of history, burdened as they are with the many possibilities for error which accompany any human endeavor; rather it is an interpretation wrought by the Holy Spirit. And this interpretation, which takes shape in what the author says and intends to say, cannot be erroneous.

Hopefully this last assertion makes it clear that the literary forms which Luke uses are in no way to be inter-

preted in an historicizing manner. If Luke, for example, is
of the firm conviction that the Gentile mission has been
set under way by God and emphatically interprets the traditional material available to him in this sense, then the
reader here encounters the real claim of the Holy Scriptures
insofar as they are God's word.

From these last statements one might get the impression
that reading the Bible is quite complicated, so complicated
in fact that one could no longer find pleasure in doing so.
One might get the impression that to do justice to God's
word, the reader must keep the many findings of modern
exegesis in mind so that he can distinguish between the extent to which the text really reflects the author's intention
and the extent to which conventional literary forms and techniques are utilized. But such a procedure would be forbidd-
ing, and not what the text calls for. In reality literary
form and intention go together. Literary form and the
author's intention can be distinguished only to a very limited
extent. Luke's intention was not to write a series of abstract theses, but to tell a story. Only in the narrative itself will the reader find what Luke intended to say (and
what God intends to say through him). Hence, the reader
should confide in the narrative and allow himself to be
guided by the flow of the text.

Reading the Bible is much like enjoying a work of art.
Everything that biblical scholars have to say about the origin, forms, theology, and author of a biblical book and
author as well as their detailed interpretation of that book,
is just like the explanations art historians give of some famous painting. Such explanations are useful and have their
place. They might even be quite necessary in certain circumstances. But all these explanations taken singly and together are not the work of art that the painting is. And
all the explanations about what the artist really intended are

still not the painting. I come to appreciate and understand the actual painting only if I get to view it, to see its colors glow, to follow its lines, to be moved by what it depicts, and to enjoy it. And this is how to get to appreciate and understand the Sacred Scriptures too.

Bibliography
of
Works Cited in the Notes

Bibliography

The abbreviations below follow R. E. Brown, J. A. Fitzmyer, and R. E. Murphy (eds.), *The Jerome Biblical Commentary*, Prentice Hall, Englewood Cliffs, N. J., 1968, pp. xxvii-xxxiv.

Abbott, W. (ed.), *The Documents of Vatican II*, America Press, N.Y., 1966.

Bauernfeind, O., *Die Apostelgeschichte*, ThHkNT 5, Leipzig, 1939.

Baur, F. C., *Paulus, der Apostel Jesu Christi: Sein Leben und Wirken, seine Briefe und seine Lehre*, Stuttgart, 1845.

Benoit, P., "Reflections on 'Formgeschichtliche Methode,'" *Jesus and the Gospel*, vol. 1, trans. B. Weatherhead, Herder and Herder, N.Y., 1973, 11-45.

Benz, E., "Paulus als Visionär: Eine vergleichende Untersuchung der Visionsberichte des Paulus in der Apostelgeschichte und in den paulinischen Briefen," *Akademie der wissenschaftem und der Literatur in Mainz*, Abhandl. d. geistes- und sozialwiss. Klasse, 1952, Wiesbaden, 1952, 77-121.

Bisping, A., *Erklärung der Apostelgeschichte*, Münster, 1866.

Brox, N., *Zeuge und Märtyrer: Untersuchungen zur frühchristlichen Zeugnis-Terminologie*, STANT 5, Munich, 1961.

Bruce, F. F., *The Acts of the Apostles; The Greek Text with Introduction and Commentary*, Tyndale Press, London, 1951. Second edition, 1952; reprinted, 1953, 1956, etc.

Büchsel, F., "*Bastazo*," *ThDNT* I, 596.

Bultmann, R., *The History of the Synoptic Tradition*, trans. J. Marsh, Harper and Row, N.Y., 1968.

————, *History and Eschatology: The Presence of Eternity*, Harper Torchbooks, N.Y., 1957.

Cadbury, H. J., "The Speeches in Acts," *Beginnings*, 5, 402-427.

Campenhausen, H. von, "Der urchristliche Apostelbegriff," *ST* 1 (1947), 96-130.

Charles, R. H., *The Apocrypha and Pseudepigrapha of the Old Testament,* II, Oxford, 1913.

Clarke, W. K. L., "The Use of the Septuagint in Acts," *Beginnings,* 2, 66–105.

Conzelmann, H., *The Theology of St. Luke,* trans. G. Buswell, Harper and Row, N.Y., 1960.

————, *Die Apostelgeschichte,* HNT 7, Tübingen, 1963.

Dibelius, M., *From Tradition to Gospel,* trans. B. L. Woolf, Charles Scribner's Sons, N.Y., n.d.

————, *Paul,* ed. and completed by W. G. Kümmel, Westminster Press, Philadelphia, 1953.

————, *Studies in the Acts of the Apostles,* ed. H. Greeven, SCM Press, London, 1956; reprinted, 1973.

Dobschütz, E. von, "Die Berichte über die Bekehrung des Paulus," *ZNW* 29 (1930), 144–147.

Dupont, J., "Le salut des gentils et la signification théologique du Livre des Actes," *NTS* 6 (1959/60), 132–155.

————, *Les Actes des Apotres,* La Sainte Bible, Paris, third printing, 1964.

Eckart, K. G., "Urchristliche Tauf- und Ordinationsliturgie (Kol 1,9–20 Act 26,18)," *Theologia Viatorum* 8 (1961/62), 23–37.

Eissfeldt, O., *Hexateuch-Synopse: Die Erzählung der fünf Bücher Mose und des Buches Josua mit dem Anfange des Richterbuches in ihre vier Quellen zerlegt,* Leipzig, 1922 (reprint: Darmstadt, 1962).

————, *The Old Testament: An Introduction,* trans. P. R. Ackroyd, Harper and Row, N.Y., 1965.

Evans, C. F., "The Kerygma," *JTS* 7 (1956) 25–41.

Felten, J., *Die Apostelgeschichte,* Freiburg, 1892.

Fitzmyer, J. A., "The Biblical Commission's Instruction on the Historical Truth of the Gospels," *TS* 25 (1964), 386–408.

Foakes-Jackson, F. J., *The Acts of the Apostles,* MNTC, London, 1931.

Gaechter, P., *Petrus und seine Zeit,* Innsbruck, 1958.

Girlanda, A., "De conversione Pauli in Actibus Apostolorum tripliciter narrata," *VD* 39 (1961), 66–81, 129–140, 173–184.

Grässer, E., "Die Apostelgeschichte in der Forschung der Gegenwart," *TRu* 26 (1960), 93-167.

Gräss, H., *Ostergeschehen und Osterberichte,* Göttingen, 1962.

Haenchen, E., "Tradition und Komposition in der Apostelgeschichte," *ZThK* 52 (1955), 205-255.

_____, *The Acts of the Apostles: A Commentary,* trans. B. Noble, G. Shinn, H. Anderson and R. McL. Wilson, Westminster Press, Philadelphia, 1971.

Hirsch, E., "Die drei Berichte der Apostelgeschichte über die Bekehrung des Paulus," *ZNW* 28 (1929), 305-312.

Jacquier, E., *Les Actes des Apôtres,* EBib, Paris, 1926.

Jüngst, J., *Die Quellen der Apostelgeschichte,* Gotha, 1895.

Klein, G., *Die zwölf Apostel: Ursprung und Gehalt einer Idee,* FRLANT 77, Göttingen, 1961.

Knabenbauer, J., *Commentarius in Actus Apostolorum,* CSS, Paris, 1899.

Knoch-Schürmann, *Bibel und Seelsorge: Grundlagen, Möglichkeiten und Formen biblisch bestimmter Seelsorge,* Werkhefte zur Bibelarbeit 1, Stuttgart, 1964.

Koch, K., *The Growth of the Biblical Tradition: The Form-Critical Method,* trans. S. M. Cupitt, Charles Scribner's Sons, N.Y., 1969.

Kümmel, W. G., *Introduction to the New Testament,* trans. A. J. Mattill Jr., Abingdon, Nashville, 1966.

_____,*Römer 7 und die Bekehrung des Paulus.* Untersuchungen zum Neuen Testament 17, Leipzig, 1929.

Lake, K., "The Conversion of Paul and the Events Immediately Following It," *Beginnings* 5, 188-195.

Lietzmann, H., *An die Korinther I, II,* HNT, Tübingen, 1949.

Lilly, J. L., "The Conversion of Saint Paul: The Validity of His Testimony to the Resurrection of Jesus Christ," *CBQ* 6 (1944), 180-204.

Linton, O., "The Third Aspect: A Neglected Point of View. A Study in Gal. 1-2 and Acts 9 and 15," *ST* 3 (1950/51), 79-95.

Lohfink, G., "Eine alttestamentliche Darstellungsform für Gotteserscheinungen in den Damaskusberichten (Apg 9; 22; 26)," *BZ* 9 (1965), 43-48.

_____, "Die Himmelfahrt Jesu im lukanischen Geschichtswerk," *BiKi* 20 (1965), 43-48.

Loisy, A., *Les Actes des Apôtres,* Paris, 1920.

Meyer, E., *Ursprung und Anfänge des Christentums, III: Die Apostelgeschichte und die Anfänge des Christentums,* Stuttgart/Berlin, 1923.

Moske, E., *Die Bekehrung des heil. Paulus: Eine exegetisch-kritische Untersuchung,* Münster, 1907.

Munck, J., *Paul and the Salvation of Mankind,* trans. F. Clarke, John Knox Press, Richmond, 1959.

Mussner, F., "'Schichten' in der paulinischen Theologie, dargetan an 1 Kor 15," *BZ* 9 (1965), 59-70.

Noth, M., *A History of the Pentateuchal Traditions,* trans. B. W. Anderson, Prentice-Hall, Englewood Cliffs, N.J., 1972.

Perk, J., *Die Apostelgeschichte: Werden und Wachsen der jungen Kirche,* Stuttgart, 1954.

Pfaff, E., *Die Bekehrung des h. Paulus in der Exegese des 20. Jahrhunderts,* Rome, 1942.

Pfister, F., "Epiphanie," *PWSup* 4, col. 277-323.

Philonenko, M., *Joseph et Asêneth: Introduction, texte critique, traduction et notes,* SPB 13, Brill, Leiden, 1968.

Prokulski, W., "The Conversion of St. Paul," *CBQ* 19 (1957), 453-473.

Rahner, K., *Visions and Prophecies,* trans. C. Henkey and R. Strachan, QD 10, Herder and Herder, N.Y., 1963.

Rigaux, B., *The Letters of St. Paul: Modern Studies,* trans. S. Yonick, Franciscan Herald Press, Chicago, 1968.

Schlatter, A., *Die Apostelgeschichte,* Erläuterungen zum Neuen Testament, part 4, Calwer Verlag, Stuttgart, 1948.

Schlier, H., *Der Brief an die Galater,* Meyer 7, Göttingen, twelfth printing, 1962.

_____, *The Relevance of the New Testament,* trans. W. J. O'Hara, Herder and Herder, N.Y., 1968.

Schmid, L., *"kentron," ThDNT III, 663-668.*

Schmid, J., *Matthäus und Lukas: Eine Untersuchung des Verhältnisses ihrer Evangelien,* BSt 23, 2–4, Freiburg, 1930.

Schnackenburg, R., "Formgeschichtliche Methode," *LTK* IV, col. 211–213.

————, *New Testament Theology Today,* trans. D. Askew, Herder and Herder, N.Y., 1963.

————, "Zur formgeschichtlichen Methode in der Evangelienforschung," *ZKT* 85 (1963), 16–32.

Schweizer, E., "Concerning the Speeches in Acts," in *Studies in Luke-Acts; Essays presented in Honor of Paul Schubert,* ed. L. E. Keck; J. L. Martyn, Abingdon, Nashville, 1966, 208–216.

Smend, F., "Untersuchungen zu den Acta-Darstellungen von der Bekehrung des Paulus," *Angelos* 1 (1925), 34–45.

Spitta, F., *Die Apostelgeschichte: Ihre Quellen und deren geschichtlicher Wert,* Halle, 1891.

Stanley, D. M., "Paul's Conversion in Acts: Why the Three Accounts?", *CBQ* 15 (1953), 315–338.

Stählin, G., *Die Apostelgeschichte,* NTD 5, Göttingen, 1962.

Steinmann, A., *Die Apostelgeschichte,* Bonn, fourth printing, 1934.

Thackeray, H. St. John, *Josephus: Jewish Antiquities I-IV,* LCL, London/Cambridge, 1957.

Trocmé, E., *Le "Livre des Actes" et l'histoire,* Paris, 1957.

Vögtle, A., "Die historische und theologische Tragweite der heutigen Evangelienforschung," *ZKT* 86 (1964), 385–417.

Vosté, J. M., "Sancti Pauli Conversio," *Ang* 8 (1931), 469–514.

Wellhausen, J., *Kritische Analyse der Apostelgeschichte.* Abhandlungen der Akademie der Wissenschaften in Göttingen, vol. 15, 2, Berlin, 1914.

Wendland, P., *Die urchristlichen Literaturformen,* HNT I, 3, Tubingen, 1913.

Wendt, H. H., *Die Apostelgeschichte,* Meyer 3, Göttingen, ninth printing, 1913.

Wikenhauser, A., *Die Apostelgeschichte und ihr Geschichtswert,* NTAbh 8, 3–5, Münster, 1921.

————, "Doppeltraume," *Bib* 29 (1948), 100–111.

————, "Die Wirkung der Christophanie vor Damaskus auf Paulus und seine Begleiter nach den Berichten der Apostelgeschichte," *Bib* 33 (1952), 313-323.

————, *New Testament Introduction*, trans. J. Cunningham, Herder and Herder, N.Y., 1958.

————, *Die Apostelgeschichte*, RNT 5, Regensburg, 1961.

Wilckens, U., "Die Bekehrung des Paulus als religionsgeschichtliches Problem" *ZThK* 56 (1959), 273-293.

————, *Die Missionsreden der Apostelgeschichte: Form- und traditionsgeschichtliche Untersuchungen*, WMzANT 5, Neukirchen-Vluyn, 1963.

Windisch, H., "Die Christusepiphanie vor Damaskus (Act 9, 22 und 26) und ihre religionsgeschichtlichen Parallelen," *ZNW* 31 (1932), 1-23.

————, *Paulus und Christus: Ein biblisch-religionsgeschichtlicher Vergleich*, Untersuchungen zum Neuen Testament 24, Leipzig, 1934.

Zahn, T., *Die Apostelgeschichte des Lucas*, Kommentar zum Neuen Testament 5, Leipzig/Erlangen, 1919/21.

Notes

Notes

These notes follow the "short title" method of citation. Full bibliographical details will be found in the BIBLIOGRAPHY above.

1. See the text in Abbott, *The Documents of Vatican II*, pp. 111-28.

2. See the text in Abbott, *The Documents of Vatican II*, pp. 137-78.

3. For a highly indignant and often petty attempt to express such misgivings and apprehensions, see *The Wanderer* 106, No. 44 (November 8, 1973) pp. 7-10. This "journalese" campaign against Catholic biblical scholars led to the publication of a "Letter to the American Bishops," *CBQ* 35 (1973) pp. 502-6, in which a group of Catholic scholars plead for understanding in face of increasing invective on the part of lay (i.e. non-professional) Catholic reactionaries.

4. This sentence means what it says. Think of how many scientific and political details are presented to non-professionals today in daily papers and weekly news magazines.

5. What this term means will be explained in what follows, especially in Chapter III, section 1, below.

6. Koch, in his important book, *The Growth of the Biblical Tradition,* explains the form-critical method by taking as examples a legal text, several Psalms, the Sermon on the Mount, and the like. But the most impressive example he chooses is "The Ancestress of Israel in Danger"- a narrative text (pp. 111-31).

7. Cf. Schnackenburg, "Zur formgeschichlichen Methode"; Vögtle, "Tragweite der heutigen Evangelien-forschung"; (both essays have further bibliography).

8. Haenchen, *Acts* p. 116.

9. Cf. Stählin, *Apostelegeschichte,* p. 133.

10. In Acts, the name "Christians" is introduced first at 11:26, and then used only once more at 26:28. Luke has many other names for the Christian community—here, for example, "those belonging to the Way."

11. Cf. 26:14, later.

12. The Greek text of 9:4 has *Saoul,* and not *Saulos* or *Paulos.* The view that Saul received the name "Paul" at his conversion simply cannot be eradicated. In reality, though, Acts says nothing at all about such a change of names. Paul had both names, and this from his childhood.

13. Cf. 22:11 and 26:13f.

14. Cf. Haenchen, *Acts,* p. 323 on v. 13.

15. The translator has rendered the Greek text and set up the parallel columns. For a more readable and more artistic translation, the reader is urged to use one of the many available published versions.

16. Cf. the essay of Mussner, " 'Schichten' in der paulinischen Theologie."

17. Cf. further Rom 1:5; 1 Cor 1:1; 2 Cor 1:1; Gal 1:1; Rom 15: 16; Phil 3:7-13; 2 Cor 4:6 (?); 5:18-20; 13:10.

18. See also Phil 3:6; Gal 1:23.

19. Note the more intense description in comparison with chs. 8,9 and 22 of Acts!

20. The translation is from the RSV.

21. Cf. also Grass, *Ostergeschehen und Osterberichte,* p. 218f.

22. Also compare 2 Cor 11:32,33 with Acts 9:24,25.

23. Cf. Schlier, *Galater,* on this passage, The relation of such community traditions to Gal and Acts is investigated by Linton in his essay, "The Third Aspect."

24. Wilckens, "Die Bekehrung des Paulus," p. 273.

25. So argues, for example, Wikenhauser, *Apostelgeschichte,* pp. 179, 181.

26. Loisy, *Actes,* p. 394: "Consequently, the light is all that Paul saw. It is the word of Christ that Saul comes to understand, which reveals to him that Jesus is in that light." For a contrary view, cf. Bisping, *Apostelegeschichte,* p. 158; Wilkenhauser, *Apostelegeschichte,* p. 108; Wendt, *Apostelgeschichte,* p. 163.

27. That Luke purposely leaves certain questions unresolved and hanging in the air is also to be observed elsewhere in Acts. For example in Acts 1:6, he does not specify which group of persons was present at the Ascension.

28. Cf. Bauernfeind, *Apostelgeschichte,* p. 12.

29. Lk 24:30,41-42; Acts 1:4; 10:41.

30. Lk 24:31, 36,51; Acts 1:9.

31. Cf. Lohfink, "Die Himmelfahrt Jesu im lukanischen Geschichtswerk," pp. 47f.

32. In the Christophany experienced by Stephen (Acts 7:55,56), the "opened heavens" indicates that the structure of this appearance is different from the Easter appearances.

33. Cf. Lietzmann, *An die Korinther,* p. 78.

34. Cf. Haenchen, *Acts,* pp. 113-116; 420.

35. On this cf. Haenchen, *Acts,* pp. 113ff; Bauernfeind, *Apostelgeschichte,* p. 12; Conzelmann, *The Theology of St. Luke,* pp. 215ff.

36. For similar general usage of the word in the N.T.: Lk 11:49; 2 Cor 8:23; Phil 2:25.

37. "Der urchristliche Apostelbegriff," p. 115.

38. Cf., e.g., 1 Cor 15:3f. and Gal 2:2.

39. Cf., e.g., 1 Cor 15,3f. and Gal 2:2.

40. *Apostelgeschichte,* p. 57.

41. *Die zwölf Apostel,* p. 146.

42. For example, Moske, *Die Bekehrung des heil. Paulus,* pp. 15f,; Pfaff, *Die Bekehrung des h. Paulus,* p. 117; Lilly, "The Conversion of St. Paul," p. 188.

43. If we label this period of Catholic research on Acts as "conservative," we do not mean the term in any derogatory sense. It simply serves as contrast. To be sure, such classifications are not always exact. For it is not seldom that we find surprisingly "modern" points of view in older works. We might also note that a whole range of "conservative" interpretation can be found among Protestants as well. —In what follows, we do not intend to present a history of the research on this problematic in Acts. The examples are simply meant to be paradigms to help clarify what we mean by "conservative" exegesis.

44. "The Conversion of St. Paul," p. 461.

45. Cf. Chapter III, section 6, below.

46. *Actus Apostolorum,* p. 161.

47. "He had St. Paul as his sole source," p. 161; cf. p. 157.

48. "He narrates (the incident) to Agrippa in compendium fashion, simultaneously including many things which were not done and said at the same time or place," p. 161; similarly, Meyer, *Anfänge des Christentums,* p. 342; Zahn, *Apostelgeschichte,* p. 799-800; Schlatter, *Apostelgeschichte,* p. 215; Felten, *Apostelgeschichte,* p. 193: "The usual and, it seems to me, the correct solution to the difficulty is that Paul expresses himself briefly before Agrippa, and therefore . . . gives a summary report of 9:3-19 and 22:6-21."

49. "Sancti Pauli Conversio," p. 498.

50. *Apostelgeschichte,* p. 91.

51. *Anfänge des Christentums,* p. 341; cf. 343; and similarly Felten, *Apostelgeschichte,* p. 194.

52. *Acts,* p. 80.

53. "Paul's Conversion in Acts," p. 325.

54. *Petrus und seine Zeit,* pp. 409-414.

55. P. 410.

56. P. 409.

57. *Homilia XLVII in Acta,* in *PG* 60, p. 153; 69, p. 328.

58. For proof, see Pfaff, *Die Bekehrung des h. Paulus,* p. 110.

59. *Acts,* p. 199.

60. Thus Moske, *Die Bekehrung des heil. Paulus,* p. 20; Wikenhauser, *Apostelgeschichte,* p. 246; Lilly, "The Conversion of St. Paul," pp. 183f.; Stählin, *Apostelgeschichte,* p. 134.

61. *Apostelgeschichte,* p. 754

62. The favorite reference to the change of grammatical case after "to hear" (*akouein*) (authors cited in Pfaff, *Die Bekehrung des h. Paulus,* p. 111) is meaningless; Luke has a penchant for variation of style. Cf. the counterarguments in Wikenhauser, "Die Wirkung der Christophanie vor Damaskus," p. 315, and in Haenchen, *Acts,* p. 322, n. 1.

63. "The Conversion of St. Paul," pp. 461-62, n. 22.

64. *Apostelgeschichte,* p. 160; likewise Felten, *Apostelgeschichte,* p. 193; Bruce, *Acts,* p. 444; Perk, *Apostelgeschichte,* p. 214; Lilly, "The Conversion of St. Paul," p. 183; Pfaff, *Die Bekehrung des h. Paulus,* pp. 108f.; and many others.

65. *Apostelgeschichte,* pp. 90f.

66. Warneck, "Pauli Bekehrung," in *Beweis des Glaubens*, 1872, p. 405; Albrecht, *Die ersten fünfzehn Jahre der christlichen Kirche*, Münster, 1900 —both cited from Moske, *Die Bekehrung des heil. Paulus*, p. 18.

67. Felten, *Apostelgeschichte*, p. 193; Knabenbauer, *Actus Apostolorum*, p. 162; Lilly, "The Conversion of St. Paul," p. 182.

68. The more recent major works on Pentateuchal criticism are Eissfeldt, *Hexateuch-Synopose* and Noth, *A History of the Pentateuchal Traditions*. An excellent survey of the problem is offered by Eissfeldt, *The Old Testament: An Introduction*. For a general view of the literary critical method, see Koch, *The Growth of the Biblical Tradition*, pp. 68-77.

69. Cf. the introductions to the N.T. on the "Synoptic question": Wikenhauser, *New Testament Introduction;* W.G. Kümmel, *Introduction to the New Testament;* and for a more extensive analysis, Schmid, *Matthäus und Lukas*.

70. *Die Apostelgeschichte*, pp. 144f.; 270-77.

71. *Die Quellen der Apostelgeschichte*, pp. 83ff.; 223ff.

72. *Die Apostelgeschichte*, pp. 166-68.

73. "Die drei Berichte der Apostelgeschichte," pp. 305-12.

74. "The Conversion of St. Paul," pp. 190f.

75. *Le "Livre des Actes,"* pp. 174-79.

76. Haenchen, *Acts*, pp. 326f.

77. On what follows, see Haenchen, *Acts*, pp. 327f.

78. It is not very helpful to consider, with Trocmé (*Le "Livre des Actes,"* p. 176), the motif of the conversion in ch. 9 as a Lukan insertion from ch. 26. Why can it not be considered an insertion in ch. 26? That would remove any reason for distinguishing sources.

79. Wendt, *Apostelgeschichte*, pp. 166ff.; Lake, "The Conversion of Paul," p. 190; Trocmé, *Le "Livre des Actes,"* p. 176: "The key to the whole problem is the episode of Ananias, absent from ch. 26."

80. Cf. already Baur, *Paulus*, second printing, 1866, I, pp. 71ff., cited from Hirsch, "Die drei Berichte der Apostelgeschichte," pp. 175f., n. 3; and especially Wendland, *Die urchristlichen Literaturformen*, pp. 328ff. and Dobschütz, "Die Berichte über die Bekehrung des Paulus." Catholic authors solved the problem by explaining that *Paul* used an abridged manner of expression in his speech. Wikenhauser ("Die Wir-

kung der Christophanie vor Damaskus," p. 314) then goes a step further: "The difference can be explained satisfactorily by the assumption that the author here—where he gives his readers a third account of what happened before Damascus—presents the content of the Apostle's speech in strongly abridged and summarized fashion."

81. Cf. Dibelius, *Studies in Acts*, p. 158, n. 47; p. 175; Haenchen, *Acts*, pp. 325-28; Conzelmann, *Apostelgeschichte*, p. 59; Stahlin, *Apostelgeschichte*, pp. 309f.

82. See especially the programmatic essay of Dibelius, "Style Criticism of the Book of Acts," in *Studies in Acts*, pp. 1-25, and Haenchen, "Tradition und Komposition."

83. Cf. Conzelmann, *Apostelgeschichte*, p. 126.

84. What this means is that where the literary critical method fails to produce convincing results, it is still possible to probe into the history of the tradition process.

85. Cf. Josephus, *Antiquities*, Prooemium 3, or Lk 1:1-4.

86. On what follows, cf. the important essay of Dibelius, "The Speeches in Acts and Ancient Historiography," in *Studies in Acts*, pp. 138-85.

87. *CIL* XIII, 1668.

88. Cf. Dibelius, *Studies in Acts*, p. 139.

89. *Antiquities*, Prooemium 3.

90. Translation from the RSV.

91. *Antiquities* I, 13, 2-3, translation by Thackeray, §§228-31.

92. *Antiquities*, Prooemium 3.

93. The following are the more important modern works on the speeches in Acts: Cadbury, "The Speeches in Acts"; Dibelius, "The Speeches in Acts and Ancient Historiography," in *Studies in Acts;* Evans, "The Kerygma"; Wilckens, *Die Missionsreden der Apostelgeschichte*. A good summary of the problems can be found in Grasser, "Die Apostelgeschichte in der Forschung der Gegenwart," pp. 133-49, and Kümmel, *Introduction to the New Testament*, pp. 112-23.

94. *Studies in Acts*, pp. 150f.; cf. also the data presented by Jacquier, *Actes*, p. CCLIX.

95. Speeches in the strict sense are lacking only in chapters 6, 8, 9, 12, 16, 18, 21, 23. But even in these passages, there are frequent citations of the words of various speakers.

96. *Apostelgeschichte,* p. 17.

97. *Studies in Acts,* p. 57; cf. also pp. 154–55.

98. "The Kergyma," p. 28.

99. Cf. also Kümmel, *Introduction to the New Testament,* p. 118.

100. More extensively in Lohfink, "Die Himmelfahrt Jesu im lukanischen Geschichtswerk."

101. The exalted Christ sends the Spirit, who endows the disciples with the ability to fulfill their tasks (cf. Lk 24:47–49; Acts 1f.).

102. Cf. especially Wilckens, *Die Missionsreden der Apostelgeschichte,* pp. 145–49; and Brox, *Zeuge und Märtyrer,* pp. 43–55.

103. The Septuagint (abbreviated, LXX, i.e., seventy in Roman numerals) is a Greek translation of the Old Testament completed about the 2nd century B.C. Aramaic is a Semitic language related to Hebrew and spoken in Palestine during the time of Jesus.

104. "In the Hebraic text of Amos 9:12 we read of the remnant of Edom, in the LXX (as the result of the mis-reading: *'adam* for *'edom*) of the remnant of men; in Acts 15:17 James says *hoi kataloipoi ton anthropon* (the remnants of men), as if he were a Jew of the Diaspora who knew only the Greek Bible," Dibelius, *Studies in Acts,* p. 179. Acts 1:20 contains a similar instance.

105. "Tradition und Komposition," p. 208.

106. Dibelius especially has often noted this literary technique of Luke's; see *Studies in Acts,* pp. 7, 57, 160.

107. Cf. Haenchen, *Acts,* p. 160, n. 4.

108. Cf. Haenchen, *Acts,* p. 629.

109. Cf. Dibelius, *Studies in Acts,* p. 106 on a similar case in Acts 15:7.

110. *Studies in Acts,* p. 165; also 153–54, 156, 158; even before Dibelius, Cadbury, "The Speeches in Acts," noted: "Like the choral passages in the Greek drama they explain to the reader the meaning of the events" (p. 402).

111. Acts 10:1–11, 17.

112. Speeches in the *strict* sense—cf. point 1 of this chapter.

113. *From Tradition to Gospel,* pp. 7–19; *Studies in Acts,* p. 111, 165.

114. "Concerning the Speeches in Acts."

115. *Die Missionsreden der Apostelgeschichte.*

116. Dibelius-Kümmel, *Paul,* p. 14: "If one compares Peter's speeches in Acts 2; 3; 10 with Paul's speech in chapter 13, one can see that the author intended to bring out the sameness of the type."—Conzelmann, *Apostelgeschichte,* p. 8: The mission speeches are intended to set forth "the substantial unity of primitive Christian, i.e., normative, preaching."

117. The fact that Luke, unlike his ancient literary contemporaries, nearly always avoids indirect speech is closely related to this *address* function.

118. Probably, for example, in the speech of Stephen.

119. Cf. Schnackenburg, *New Testament Theology Today,* pp. 48-49.

120. The form-critical method (*formgeschichtliche Methode*) was programmatically developed for New Testament study by Dibelius (*From Tradition to Gospel,* original German publication date 1919) and Bultmann (*The History of the Synoptic Tradition,* original German publication date 1921). It is not my intention to present this program of study and its history here. For this, see Schnackenburg, "Formgeschichtliche Methode" (short outline, bibliography), Benoit, "Reflections on 'Formgeschichtliche Methode'" (critique), and Koch, *The Growth of the Biblical Tradition* (examples, terminology). I would just like to note here, that from its beginnings, form-criticism was mainly concerned with the forms and normative patterns of *oral* tradition. "In these cases our enquiry is not directed towards the personality of the authors, nor towards their literary dexterity" (Dibelius, *From Tradition to Gospel,* p. 7). But from about 1950, form-critics extended their scope to include *literary* forms and patterns as well. They study these patterns in New Testament texts to find out how the N.T. authors shaped the tradition (this study is called redactional or editorial criticism, *Redaktionsgeschichte*). With this further development of the method, it became possible to delve into the fuller history of the tradition process (*Traditionsgeschichte*), and with it, Acts becomes an interesting area of form-critical research.

The first to apply form-critical perspectives to Acts in a methodically conscious way was Dibelius. Significantly, the work which launched the series of his essays on Acts in 1923 (collected in 1951 in his *Studies in Acts*) bore the title: "*Style Criticism* of the Book of Acts." His approach still presupposed the original and narrower idea of form-criticism. Haenchen then assimilated the essays of Dibelius into his commentary on Acts, further developed them and brought the method to the general awareness of most exegetes. On the Catholic side, there is still no major commentary on Acts in which form-critical considerations are applied.

121. §38: "Hence the Catholic commentator, in order to comply with the present needs of biblical studies . . . should also make a prudent use of this means, determine, that is, to what extent the manner of expression or the literary mode adopted by the sacred writer may lead to a correct and genuine interpretation; and let him be convinced that this part of his office cannot be neglected without serious detriment to Catholic exegesis." (Cited from the National Catholic Welfare Conference translation, Washington, 1943, p. 19. The encyclical was issued in September, 1943.)

122. §X. "Unless the exegete pays attention to all these things which pertain to the origin and composition of the Gospels and makes proper use of all the laudable achievements of recent research, he will not fulfill his task of probing into what the sacred writers intended and what they really said." (Cited from Fitzmyer, "The Biblical Commission's Instruction," p. 406. The Instruction was issued in May, 1964.)

123. §12. "Those who search out the intention of the sacred writers must, among other things, have regard for 'literary forms.' For truth is proposed and expressed in a variety of ways, depending on whether a text is history of one kind or another, or whether its form is that of prophecy, poetry, or some other type of speech. The interpreter must . investigate what meaning the sacred writer intended to express and actually expressed in particular circumstances as he used contemporary literary forms in accordance with his own time and culture. For the correct understanding of what the sacred author wanted to assert, due attention must be paid to the customary and characteristic styles of perceiving, speaking and narrating which prevailed at the times of the sacred writer, and to the customs men normally followed at that period in their everyday dealings with one another." (Cited from Abbott, *The Documents of Vatican II*, p. 120. The Dogmatic Constitution on Revelation was issued in November, 1965.)

124. For a more extensive explanation of the following material, see Lohfink, "Eine alttestamentliche Darstellungsform," pp. 246–57.

125. More thoroughly, see Lohfink, "Eine altestamentliche Darstellungsform," pp. 248–49.

126. Namely Gen 46:2 and Ex 3:4; exception: Gen 31:11.

127. The Greek text of "Joseph and Aseneth" is translated as literally as possible from the edition of Philonenko, *Joseph et Asêneth*, pp. 176 and 178.

128. For example: Gen 12:1-3; 15:1-5; 17:1ff.; 28:12-15; 3 Kings 19:9ff.; Is 6; Ezech 1f.

129. Thus most recently Trocmé, Le *"Livre des Actes,"* pp. 177-178; Haenchen, *Acts,* pp. 322, 686; Stählin, *Apostelgeschichte,* p. 310.

130. In ch. 9, God readies his plan with the presentation of the future great missionary to the Gentiles as "chosen instrument" (9:15). In ch. 10 God launches the Gentile mission through Peter. On this interpretation of ch. 10, see Dibelius, *Studies in Acts,* pp. 114-117; Haenchen, *Acts,* pp. 362-63.

131. *Apostelgeschichte,* p. 136.

132. "These elements, repeated three times, in some way give basis to the reality of the fact, and therefore they are entirely essential. The other elements which are found in individual passages or are proper to two only, concern us even more so because in them the hand of the author appears, and from them we learn how he understood the fact" (p. 75).

133. Cf. Chapter II, Section 1 above.

134. Gaechter, *Petrus und seine Zeit,* p. 409.

135. Clarke, "The Use of the Septuagint in Acts," pp. 99-100 presents a synoptic table of the respective Acts and Septuagint texts.

136. Cf. Wikenhauser, *Apostelgeschichte,* p. 272.

137. Cf. Chapter III, section 1, point 7, above.

138. See Chapter III, section 8 below.

139. Most recently, Trocmé, Le *"Livre des Actes,"* p. 177.

140. *Paul and the Salvation of Mankind,* p. 26.

141. Haenchen, *Acts,* p. 686: "early Christian edificatory language"; Conzelmann, *Apostelgeschichte,* p. 139: "edificatory language of the Christian community"; Stählin, *Apostelgeschichte,* p. 308: "the language of early Christian mission."

142. Eckart, "Urchristliche Tauf- und Ordinations-liturgie," even intends to show that Acts 26:18 is a passage formed previously in tradition, which conceals a primitive Christian "ordination liturgy for conversion and baptism" (p. 37). It seems to me that he does not really prove his point, although it is possible.

143. Haenchen, *Acts,* p. 175.

144. For the difference between "form" and "motif," see Koch,

The Growth of the Biblical Tradition, pp. 56–57.

145. Wikenhauser, "Doppelträume."

146. He could have referred to the preparatory work of Smend, "Untersuchungen zu den Acta-Darstellungen von der Bekehrung des Paulus," pp. 37–38, and Wendland, *Die urchristlichen Literaturformen,* pp. 327f.

147. Pap. Oxyrh. XI, 1381, col IIff.; the following is a literal translation, following the text in Wikenhauser, "Doppelträume," pp. 106–7.

148. The god Asklepios is meant here.

149. Cf. Smend, "Untersuchungen," pp. 37f.; Haenchen, "Tradition und Komposition," p. 214. I consider Josephus, who likewise evidences this motif, a Hellenistic author.

150. Cf. Haenchen, *Acts,* pp. 357–59; Benz, "Paulus als Visionär," pp. 83, 88.

151. For example, Peter's vision in 10:9–16; thus Conzelmann, *Apostelgeschichte,* pp. 61f. correctly against Haenchen, *Acts,* pp. 361f.

152. Kümmel wrote a fundamental essay against the psychologizing of the Damascus appearance in his, "Römer 7 und die Bekehrung des Paulus"; especially see pp. 154–57.

153. Aeschylus, *Agamemnon,* 1624; *Prometheus,* 322ff.; Euripides, *Bacchantes,* 795. Further examples and extensive bibliography in Schmid, "*kentron,*" pp. 663–68.

154. Cf. Schmid, "*kentron,*" pp. 664f.

155. Cf. further, the interesting work of Rahner, *Visions and Prophecies,* which unfortunately has not been noted by many N.T. scholars.

156. Cf. Haenchen, *Acts,* p. 691.

157. See Chapter III, section 2, above.

158. *Light:* Lk 2:9; 24:4; Acts 12:7; Ezech 1:13, 27,28; Dan 7: 9f.; 10:6; 4 Macc 4:10; eth. Enoch 14:22; 71:2, 5f.; slav. Enoch 1:5; 20:1; Apocalypse of Abraham 8:2; 19:1; 15:6; 17:1; and many other passages. For Hellenism, see Pfister, "Epiphanie," cols 315,316.
Falling down: e.g., Ezech 1:28; 44:4; 2 Macc 3:27; Jubilees 15:5; eth. Enoch 60:3; slav. Enoch 21:2; Apocalypse of Sophonia 8:4; other passages are collected by Wikenhauser, "Die Wirkung der Christophanie vor Damaskus."

159. For examples, see Wikenhauser, "Die Wirkung der Christophanie

vor Damaskus," pp. 316–22.

160. Translation from RSV.

161. See F. Nötscher, *Das Buch Daniel*, EB, p. 645, n. 7.

162. Haenchen, *Acts*, p. 322; Baur, *Paulus*, p. 68 already stated this well; cf. further Wendt, *Apostelgeschichte*, p. 164; Schlatter, *Apostelgeschichte*, p. 193; Pfaff, *Die Bekehrung des h. Paulus*, p. 112; Conzelmann, *Apostelgeschichte*, p. 58.

163. The question of the details involved in the literary-psychological process in Luke is still open. It is variously explained by Wikenhauser, "Die Wirkung der Christophanie vor Damaskus," p. 315; Haenchen, *Acts*, p. 321, no. 7; Conzelmann, *Apostelgeschichte*, p. 59.

164. *Le "Livre des Actes,"* pp. 176f.

165. Thus also Dibelius, *From Tradition to Gospel*, pp. 204f.; Koch, *The Growth of the Biblical Tradition*, pp. 199–200; Benoit, "Reflections on 'Formgeschichtliche Methode,'" pp. 43ff.

166. For a better and more extensive consideration of the structure of history and the nature of historical knowledge, see Bultmann, *History and Eschatology*, pp. 123–37; the best treatment of the subject of literary technique and composition and history is to be found in Schlier, "What is Meant by the Interpretation of Scripture," in *The Relevance of the New Testament*, pp. 39–75; on our question see especially pp. 44f., 47f., and 56–59; and Koch, *The Growth of the Biblical Tradition*, pp. 155–58, offers some important considerations relative to sagas in the Bible.

167. The phrase translates the German, "Richtungssinn," a term coined by Dibelius, *Studies in Acts*, pp. 114, 119, (where the English translation has "meaning of the version," and "version (of Luke) is aiming at.").

168. See Chapter I, section 2, above.

169. *Kritische Analyse der Apostelgeschichte*, p. 17; likewise Wendland, *Die urchristlichen Literaturformen*, p. 329.

170. Bauernfeind, *Apostelgeschichte*, p. 129; Trocmé, *Le "Livre des Actes"*, p. 175.

171. On the questions Luke faced and the answers he gave to them, see especially Dibelius, *Studies in Acts*, pp. 160f., 169f.; Haenchen, *Acts*, pp. 90ff., 99f., 128f., 328, 629f.; J. Dupont, "Le salut de gentils," pp. 135f., 141, 150f., 155.

172. Acts 22:3; 26:4f.

Notes

173. Acts 9:1f., 13f., 21; 22:4f., 19f.; 26:9-11.

174. Cf. the following chapter!

175. Cf. Haenchen, *Acts*, pp. 100-101.

176. The exceptions are Ex 3:2-10 and the vision of Ananias in Acts 9:10f.

177. Cf. Chapter III, section 4, above.

178. Thus Windisch, *Paulus und Christus,* pp. 137f.; Stanley, "Paul's Conversion in Acts," pp. 334, 338; Girlanda, "De conversione Pauli," p. 138.

179. Cf. Chapter III, section 3, above.

180. The value Luke placed upon the idea that the Gentile mission belongs to the O.T. promises is shown by Lk 24:44-47 and Acts 26:22f. On this, see especially Dupont, "Le salut de gentils," pp. 150f.

181. Haenchen, *Acts,* on chap. 22 (p. 629): "It would have been a serious literary error if Luke had once again brought in the account of Chapter 9, merely changing the third person to the first."

182. We should also treat of the stylistic-grammatical variants here, but this can only be seen on the basis of the Greek text.

183. "Die drei Berichte der Apostelgeschichte über die Bekehrung des Paulus," p. 310.

184. Cf. Loisy, *Actes,* p. 394.

185. This passage belongs to the narrative context of the first account; see Chapter I, section 1, above.

186. In Greek, the word "I" (*ego*) is emphasized.

187. This Lukan intensification of Paul's activity as persecutor is well described by Klein, *Die Zwölf Apostel,* pp. 115-27. But Klein concludes that Luke's aim was to disparage the figure of Paul (p. 144), and this is quite false.

188. Exception: Conzelmann, *Apostelgeschichte.*

189. The reasons for this interpretation: 1) the Greek *enopion* (lit.: *before*) in Luke means "in the presence of" and answers the question "where, in what place" (31 times); there are extremely few places where this word would mean "where to, to, toward," at most Luke 5:18; Acts 6:5; 10:30; 2) the word *gar* (English "for" gives the reason for the previous statement) in v. 16 can be adequately understood only if "before" means "in the presence of" here; 3) it is quite possible

that the background to the formulation of this statement is the tradition contained in Lk 21:12-19, cf. especially 21:12, 17!; 4). "to bear the name" (*bastazein onoma*) is a Greek idiom meaning "to confess, profess," see Büchsel, "*Bastazo*," p. 596, n. 7.

190. For example, situations as described in Acts 16:19-24; 18:12f.; 21:27-22:22; 22:30-23:6; 24:1-21; 25:6-12; 25:23-26:32.

191. Cf. Bauernfeind, *Apostelgeschichte*, pp. 129f.

192. Cf. in the first place, the superscriptions: Rom 1:1; 1 Cor 1:1; 2 Cor 1:1; then 1 Cor 9:1-3; 15:9-11; Gal 1:1-2:14.

193. For that matter, this mission charge is not set down in one single formulation, as for example in Mt 28:19f. or Jn 20:21-23; rather it is presented in various stages. First, the apostles receive the command to remain in Jerusalem. There Christ sends the Holy Spirit upon them; the Spirit then equips them for the office and function of witness (cf. Lk 24:47-49; Acts 1:4, 8; 2:33).

194. The exalted Christ sends the Spirit not only in John, but also in Luke; cf. Lk 24:49; Acts 2:33.

195. Cf. Lohfink, "Die Himmelfahrt Jesu im lukanischen Geschichtswerk."

196. Luke's outline of events has both a temporal as well as a spatial dimension. Luke has purposely left out the tradition about the appearances in Galilee (compare Lk 24:6f. with Mk 16:7), and in this way Jerusalem becomes the *spatial* symbol of the continuity between Jesus and the Church. For this reason as well, Paul's call cannot be counted among the Easter appearances because it did not take place in Jerusalem.

197. Acts 13:1-4 provides an excellent possibility for comparing the abridgment and intensification of statements in ch. 26 and the rest of the accounts. According to 13:2 the Holy Spirit introduces the whole event, then the sending forth of Paul and Barnabas occurs through men, while in v. 4 the whole thing is so formulated that the entire sending forth takes place through the Spirit. Thus Acts 9 and 22 relate to 26 just like Acts 13:1-3 to 13:4.

198. Haenchen, *Acts*, pp. 127, 328,332.